D0855655

Before Addiction:
How to Help Youth

Before Addiction:
How to Help Youth

Florence Lieberman, D. S. W.
Phyllis Caroff, D. S. W.
Mary Gottesfeld, M. S. S.

WITHDRAWN
IOWA STATE UNIVERSITY
LIBRARY

Behavioral Publications
New York
1973

Library of Congress Catalog Number 73-7803
Standard Book Number 87705-112-7
Copyright © 1973 by Behavioral Publications

All rights reserved. No part of this work may be reproduced
or utilized in any form or by any means, electronic or
mechanical, including photocopying, microfilm and recording,
or by any information storage and retrieval system without
permission in writing from the publisher.

BEHAVIORAL PUBLICATIONS,
2852 Broadway—Morningside Heights,
New York, New York 10025

Printed in the United States of America
This printing 10 9 8 7 6 5 4 3 2 1

Library of Congress Cataloging in Publication Data

Lieberman, Florence.
  Before addiction: how to help youth.

  Bibliography: p. 117
  1. Drugs and youth.   2. Parent and child.
3. Counseling.   I. Caroff, Phyllis, joint author.
II. Gottesfeld, Mary, joint author.   III. Title.
[DNLM: 1. Drug addiction—In adolescence—Popular
works.   2. Drug addiction—Prevention and control—
Popular works. WM270 L714b 1973]
HV5801.L52 613.8 73-7803

HV5801
L52

Table of Contents

950841

Introduction

This book is addressed to parents, as it should be, because parents are the ones who worry most about the problem of drug use by their children. They are also the few who really want to know what they can do *before* addiction.

In this book, therefore, we are talking directly to you, the parents of adolescents today.

We are three social workers who probably came to our interest very much the same way you did, out of our concern for the children and young adolescents with whom we were working.

Several years ago, we noticed that drug use was becoming so common that we began to assume that every young person who felt troubled enough to seek some psychological help or whom somebody else referred for help because they worried about his behavior, must have had some experience with drugs. We did not know much about the problem, not even enough to realize when an adolescent was nodding on drugs. We soon learned.

Now the problem has increased in size. It is no longer confined to the large cities. Today many diverse segments of the adolescent population are involved with drugs. In fact, drug-using adolescents are now a much larger group than those who are defined as troubled and who already are in some form of treatment. Of course, the young adolescent is not the only drug-user, but this book is concerned with the young user who does not have the life experience or foresight to project into the future the consequences of drug use.

This book came about because we began to worry about these young adolescents, just as you are. At first we tried to find out what others had to say. We soon discovered that there was a wholesale seduction going on. This seduction involved how the problem was seen and what concerned everybody.

When people talk about drugs, they talk about addiction and they talk about crime. Both have received a great deal of attention. There has been little attention—too little—paid to the adolescent who is not yet addicted, and to the question of how to help him.

Even the professionals have been seduced by the issue. Either they forget to check on any drug use whenever they see young people or they spend all their time advising how to "treat" addicts.

We don't want to wait that long. We prefer to do something before addiction. As the result of some talking, thinking, and working, we wrote some papers as communications to our colleagues, hoping they would join with us in our concern. But none of that seemed enough to us, because we knew from our work with parents how worried you were. We also did not like some of the confusion we saw around us, which too often, we felt, worked to your disadvantage and to your child's.

We hoped that maybe we could be of some service if we spoke directly to you. That's how this book came to be.

As we tried to understand the present-day problems for adolescents and their parents, we found we were asking many questions, many of them probably like the questions you have been asking. For example, we asked: Why are so many young people involved in activities that are physically, socially, and psychologically detrimental to their lives? Why are their parents unable to stop them? Why are there families in which mothers and fathers are together, the homes adequate, and the children cared for, that have children who are turning on and tuning out?

We also wondered what help, if any, these families were getting from professionals, what kind, and how successful. We thought of what could be improved and how.

Finally, we asked: Is there something in modern living that is causing these difficulties? Is there something special about being young today? Is there a difference between today and yesterday?

There are three parts to this book, in which we try to deal with these questions. In the first part we talk about the problem and some of the dilemmas it poses for you. In the second, we try to offer some suggestions. The last part is concerned with social and philosophical issues and tries to explain some of the broader concerns that led to the writing of the book.

Mostly we are trying to talk to parents in the cause of their children and other people's children. We see it as only the beginning of an attempt to come to grips with some of the issues and problems *before* addiction.

Part I
Youth and Drugs

1. The Adolescent and Drugs

You probably have a gut feeling that using drugs is bad for your adolescent. But you can't help doubting that feeling if you live in today's world.

When your child was a baby, the chances are that Dr. Benjamin Spock's book *Baby and Child Care* was something you wouldn't have done without because it helped you feel confident about so many things. It wasn't just that he told you what to do in many everyday circumstances: He was also helpful in relation to emergencies. But the best contribution Dr. Spock made was to help you to relax and to feel that the first thing you must do in order to be a good parent was trust yourself and have confidence in what you were doing and feeling.

In 1972 Dr. Spock ran for president of the United States on a platform that included a call for the legalization of marijuana. What do you say when your child, now fifteen, reminds you of that?

Then there are some very well-written books, the products of reputable and well-thought-of professionals, that extol drug use as the source of almost religious benefits. Not only are drugs pleasurable, according to these books; drugs also expand consciousness and lead the user toward enlightenment. Similar discussions on television feature important, articulate men.

Probably you have discussed the use of drugs with your friends at many cocktail parties and over many dinners. Perhaps some of your friends, or you yourself, have used some drugs and have discussed these experiences, some of which were probably enjoyable and even "enlightening."

3

Can you ignore these facts, arguments, and experiences when you speak to your child about drugs and your feeling that he should not use them? Of course not.

But, in fact, most of the arguments for drugs are made by adults and apply to adults—no one else. With respect to marijuana or hallucinogenic drugs, the argument is that they "expand consciousness." What this means is that they may change your perception of the world. A good case can be made for the value of such an experience for someone stuck in his ways—someone who has developed a too-rigid view of the world, someone who has been lulled into a routine way of seeing things. Most of us would probably agree that it is sometimes good to re-evaluate one's views. Some say that these drugs could help do that. At least it is debatable.

But who can say that an adolescent has become stuck in his ways—that he has become lulled in a routine? He hasn't had enough time. In fact, the task of adolescence may be to develop just such a routine, a worldview, or what has come to be called an "identity."

Adolescence is the very time a person must begin to develop his path in the world, to learn about himself as an individual, to develop a wide view of the world, and so on. And he must do this faced with frightening new life-dimensions and demands: in school, in learning to handle money, in growing and other physical factors, and perhaps most important, with respect to sex.

These are fast-changing times, and it is hard to get an unblurred view of the world. Just what any adolescent doesn't need at this time is an artificial outside agent further altering his outlook. Nor does he need a cloud of smoke around his head to block his view. No, this adolescent is not the same as a disgruntled middle-ager set in his ways.

Regardless of the benefits or harm drug use may entail, some of your friends, and authors and commentators, may argue that a person should be free to choose what he wants to do. This can be an argument used in support of the legalization of drugs, even heroin, however deadly it may be. A good argument can be made for a person's right to kill himself.

Now, when this argument is applied to adults, it is debatable. The adult is, by definition, responsible for himself. And—there is no getting around it—there is a double standard, because the adolescent, by definition, is not yet totally responsible for himself. Therefore, he cannot have the same rights and privileges as an independent adult. Adolescence represents movement toward independence, toward more responsibility.

It is during this time that the adolescent is learning to control his life, that he is moving increasingly out of the home, out of his family, and into the community, be it only his community of friends. But usually the adolescent is living at home; he is not on his own. He does not make his own decisions all by himself, if only because he simply doesn't have his own living quarters. Though this shouldn't enslave him, it is an important restraint.

As you know, the sexual revolution got one of its biggest boosts when cars became available and provided a place away from home. But cars usually became available to an adolescent only when his parents gave him one. It is the same with drugs. An adolescent is less likely to venture into a first experience with drugs right in his own home when his parents are around.

Thus your adolescent is not totally free to do something that hurts him. And while he is in your house, you're not going to let him.

The simple fact is that during adolescence, children feel and act crazy enough; they do not need outside substances to make them worse!

This is the basic reason your gut feeling about drugs and adolescence is right.

WHEN IS ADOLESCENCE

This period called adolescence is a long time. Children of ten and almost-adult twenty-year-olds are both called adolescents. Now when you think about your child at ten, you know you still considered him little. Probably you expected him to do only what a child might reasonably be able to do. Because he still needed caring for, you could demand only limited responsibility from him, both for himself and for others. When he is twenty, you will expect much more. You will expect that he will have more knowledge, more strength, and have ability to take complete care of himself. Even at that age you know he still will be irresponsible in some ways and will need some help at times from other adults. However, he certainly should be able to take on many more responsibilities and to be more independent than a ten-year-old. There is a big difference between ten and twenty.

Actually, from about ten to twelve, children are commonly thought of as preadolescents, because they are not really adolescents in the physical sense, though many are beginning. This is when they seem to try to imitate the adolescents around them. Girls and boys can be very annoying. Although they spend hours before the mirror and do all kinds of things to their hair, (even boys today are very concerned about the cut and length of their hair), they rarely worry about cleanliness, personal or otherwise.

It is about this time, just when they go into junior high school or even before, that you may think you have an adolescent on your hands. That's because they suddenly become interested in the opposite sex, even though just a short time ago, girls played with girls and boys with boys, exclusively. This is one time when a lot of adults confuse these children by having inappropriate expectations for them in relation to their social readiness. Noting how they seem to talk about boyfriends and girl-friends, you may think they are involved with each other in a grownup sexual way, and you may worry about that, too. You might need to worry if you encourage the "sex-uality" by facilitating and suggesting proms, socials, and dating.

For example, Jimmy was a twelve-year-old boy, small for his age and not as grownup as most children his age. As a result he always played with younger children. That summer he went to sleepaway camp for the first time. He hadn't been very happy about going and had been quite homesick the first week, making a lot of trou-ble about wanting to go home. However, he was helped to stay for two more weeks. When he came home, he talked about having a girlfriend and began to write letters to her. His parents were very pleased and took this as a sign that he was finally growing up. They encouraged him to talk about his girlfriend and suggested ways for the two to get together. Somehow, Jimmy always had an excuse, and a meeting never occurred.

Of course, there are situations where parents are suc-cessful in getting their kids to act more grownup. Only a few years ago, *Life* magazine had pictures of a group of not-yet-teenagers lying around in each other's arms with full compliance of their parents. They had quickly grown beyond the titillation of spin-the-bottle.

What these young preteenagers need is an opportunity to talk, tease each other, and joke, and to be allowed in thought and by tentative activities to prepare for the more serious and responsible relationships of a later and more appropriate time.

Children have a great deal to do before they become men and women. They also need some preparation for adolescence, during which they become men and women. A good preparation for all the physical and emotional changes is a good and calm life within the protection of

their families and schools. When they have too many up-
sets and insecurities before they become adolescents, and
if they are pushed to perform and be grownup too fast,
adolescence itself will be very difficult. In adolescence,
too, they still need protection.

THE PHYSICAL PART OF ADOLESCENCE

The changes of adolescence are startling: physical,
emotional, intellectual, and social. You probably remember how fast the changes came about when your child
was an infant. In his teen years you are surely observing
that they are even more dramatic.

The most obvious signs are physical. These have their
impetus from hormonal secretions controlled by the central nervous system and programmed by the nature of
the human being. This physical development is basically
in the service of sex and the full-grown sexual functioning of a man or a woman.

Girls begin earlier than boys, some of them as early as
ten years of age. There have been cases of even younger
children starting to mature, but these are less common.
The first signs are little breasts, and then pubic and un-
derarm hair, contouring of hips, and menstruation. By
twelve or thirteen the majority of girls have begun these
changes. Boys, starting about twelve or thirteen, get
deeper voices, penis growth, semen ejaculation, and
pubic and facial hair. Of course all these things don't
happen at the same time. But, once started, they keep
coming in a familiar pattern.

When anyone begins to change depends upon his race,
his family patterns, his diet, and even his psychological
development. In any case, you know all about the differences in appearance and growth of a group of children
between eleven and thirteen.

Throughout the early part of adolescence this great
variation continues, some developing later and some earlier than most of their friends and classmates. Either

way, it can be worrisome for the child and his parents. For example there was Betty, a ten-year-old, who menstruated and who had large breast development. Both the girls and the boys in her class poked fun at her. They called her "Busty" and "Betty Bosom," they drew pictures of her, and the boys looked at her a lot. For her the sudden change from breastless to breasty was overwhelming. She came home crying every day, walked stooped over, trying to hide her new encumbrances. Besides having an unfamiliar body almost overnight and being different from her friends, she really had less time than they to talk and giggle and learn with them about becoming a woman.

Jack was five foot two at twelve, and almost six foot when he was thirteen. In addition, he gained enough weight so that he looked "built." Seventeen-year-old girls used to try to interest him, and he had to stoop to talk to most of his old friends. Jack seemed very depressed to his family. He seemed not to know what to do with his hands and feet. He looked years older than his friends, and in class with them it seemed as if he must have been left back. Wherever he went people treated him as if he were an adult. Jack was most unhappy because he didn't know which he was himself.

Then there's the girl who matures slowly. She feels different because her menstrual period occurs much later than her friends and as a result she continues to look and to be treated like a little girl. A late-developing boy may feel left behind by his taller, beginning-to-be-bearded friends. There is even a problem for boys in relation to when they are old enough to look as if they need to shave. For some it comes too early, and for others it seems as if it will never happen. As the parent, you know all will come in due time. But children can't know this as comfortably as you do. This is one of the problems of adolescence: When is the right time? It is sometimes very frustrating for them—and also for you.

GROWING AND FEELING

One of the problems of so much growing is getting used to the feeling of not being little any more and having a different kind of body. After all, suddenly the body of the adolescent not only looks different: It also acts and feels different. No matter how much you've told your child, and how much he knows, he is bound to have some reaction to the first involuntary nocturnal emission (wet dream) and she to the first menstrual period. There is a lot of difference between intellectual knowing and emotional experiencing.

Some adolescents seem to grow overnight; some of them even seem to feel themselves grow. Adjusting to this and to new feelings is a difficult job. It takes time for feelings and emotion to catch up to the body, and along the way there are a lot of anxieties and frustrations. After all, no adolescent is ever sure that he will make it. And waiting and using the time to learn how to manage things and to solve problems is not easy.

The adolescent who uses drugs interferes with his feeling, and he never learns what he really feels. Maybe using drugs and getting "high" temporarily help him to bypass some of the struggles that are a natural part of being adolescent. Drugs can keep him from feeling uncomfortable, from finding out how to overcome the discomfort, or from even knowing that this discomfort will pass. Drugs can be stultifying.

Adolescent drug-users learn nothing during their adolescence. They become adults knowing no more than when they were children. In fact, chronic drug-users usually are petulant, immature, and depressed. They end up emotionally retarded and emotionally damaged by artificial experiences.

Henry is a good example of this. According to his parents, he was no trouble in grade school: Henry did his homework, more or less, had some friends, and was a pretty good student. When he was fourteen he shot up, but no more than anyone else. It just happened overnight. Now, in school he found there were bigger and better boys than he, that is, he wasn't as smart as he always thought he was. To feel better about himself, he began to hang around with the boys who had always done worse than he in school. He began playing hookey from school, and in that time smoked marijuana. It got so that he was in a perpetual fog—a smokey, marijuana-induced fog. He never knew what was going on in the world; he never read a newspaper; he didn't know what was going on in school; he was an absolute bore of a kid. He slept away his time.

The worst thing about Henry was that he didn't even know how he felt—not about anything. He didn't worry about how badly he was doing in school and the fact that he eventually couldn't graduate, because whenever he began to feel anxious about being found out, he stayed home and smoked. The only emotion he ever felt was anger, and that was at his parents because they bothered him. He didn't wonder about his future, dream great dreams, or plan big things. He just went on living.

This also happened to Charles, but he was older. He was nineteen when he failed his first year in college. Because of that, his parents started him in therapy. At this time he was smoking pot heavily, several times a day. Even though he had many pleasing and extroverted qualities, he had trouble in making friends of either sex. Even though he had done well enough to get into college, once there he couldn't do the work. When he was home he just didn't get along with his family.

His difficulties had started when he began college. Then he felt he was on his own, and this made him anxious—he just wasn't ready to be even that independent. He discovered marijuana when it was used in the dorm.

Before long he was keeping to himself and engaging in four to six hours of solitary smoking. In fact, he wasted his first year in college and learned nothing from time and experience, nor did he develop emotionally. He was so afraid of feeling any discomfort that he smoked his time away. He lost that year of his life.

Once he was in treatment he was helped to talk about all the things that made him anxious: his fears of being sexually inadequate, his feelings of intellectual inferiority, and his loneliness away from home. Now that he was able to feel his discomfort, he was helped to figure out ways to overcome it. In so doing, he began to grow up, and became more independent and more interesting. He also eliminated his drug use, entered another school, and completed his education.

Henry, on the other hand, graduated to bigger and better drugs. He went through speed and LSD. Finally he became a heroin addict. Then he went to another type of school to unlearn how to undo this. You see, it wasn't enough for Henry to be stultified by marijuana. As time went on, even Henry didn't like how things were going along. So instead of learning how to manage his life, he just decided to see things differently. He became a big success, pushing and using drugs and outfoxing the cops, for a while. Then his parents had to bail him out.

INDEPENDENCE

You must have observed that though adolescence begins with biology, it ends with psychology. To become a functioning adult, your child must eventually be able to live without you. To do this, he has to feel comfortable with himself and secure. The psychology of independence is very much related to a lot of other things that develop gradually.

You usually grant him certain privileges that move

this independence along, that gradually help him learn to do things away from you and to make decisions for and by himself. Society has also programmed the different ages at which certain things can be undertaken. For example, there are driver's licenses and driving lessons, work permits and jobs, dating and more lenient curfews. These all help him to do many new things and recognize his changing status.

But the using and wanting of this independence is erratic and even troublesome. You must have experienced rebellion and complaints over demands for more freedom than you think wise. One day your child may say he is old enough to live without you and the next he may wrestle on the floor with his kid brother or tease his sister. Your daughter may talk about being in love and, right after that, fight about who got more ice cream for dessert!

Separating from and preparing to leave one's family isn't easy. It is never accomplished without some mixed feelings and some wish to remain with all the pleasures and security of childhood. In fact, the moodiness of adolescence is a kind of mourning over having to lose you in order to be independent. This is surprising to contemplate, considering how often you and your values have been ridiculed by your children. But the adolescent is really ambivalent: To stay with you is to be a kid; to be independent and away from you is scary. So the beginning of independence also entails cutting parents down in size, by denigrating their authority and still staying with them. But it is also another preparation for being independent.

The drug-user tends to be unable to tolerate the possibility of not always having his parents to take care of him, but because of his age he cannot acknowledge or even allow himself to feel this. Instead he pretends to be grownup and independent by dreaming through drugs— drugs often purchased with the allowance you gave him.

PEERS

One way of becoming independent of parents is to become dependent upon friends—then the young adolescent doesn't have to do everything by himself. He has someone with whom to talk, walk, and think—someone who is not his parent.

Of course peers are important throughout life, but there is no time of life when it is as important to have people just your age. A year or two difference, and sometimes more, doesn't make much of a difference at any other time. Even in childhood it is possible for kids of a variety of ages to get along. In early adolescence, because what you can do and what you want to do changes so quickly, age differences matter.

One way friends—particularly a group of friends—help is in finding out what other people, who matter, think. In actuality, it is a way of broadening a life's experience. The adolescent hears of ways of doing things other than the way he had been taught. He also can compare notes with his friends about his feelings, and sometimes his fears. Also, as he has to learn to get along with different people, he learns how to control himself because of others, and also has an opportunity to experiment with different aspects of himself. That's why he may have so many different kinds of friends at the beginning. They all offer different ways of being and doing. He also has the opportunity, as he gets a little older, to establish a deep and confiding relationship with one best friend with whom he shares everything.

Adolescents also share their parents. They seem to switch parents. You must have discovered that your child has a friend who seems to come to the house to talk to you, because you are so much more understanding than his parents. Well, if you look into it, you may find that your son is visiting and talking with his friend's parents.

The truth is that peers are not enough. The trouble is that collectively and individually they share the same confusions and the same riot of feelings. All young people need some adult clarification and support in their process of becoming independent. If their own parents can't help, maybe some other adult will do.

A young adolescent girls' group was meeting regularly with an adult leader. They regularly shared criticisms of all the adults they knew: their parents, their teachers, even their aunts and uncles. They criticized them for not understanding *them,* for not understanding their husbands and wives, and for being immature. Finally, in one session when the criticism of adults was more intense than ever, the leader asked whether she should be at their meetings; after all, she was an adult. The young girls replied that they needed her "or there would be a riot."

Now you know very well that peers, particularly in groups, may be good for your youngster, but they may also be bad. One thing is sure: They are influential. The adolescent is not yet in a position to be his own man, and he is extremely vulnerable to group pressure. You must hear, and frequently, about what the gang thinks and does. But do you remember that sometimes he may feel pressured by the group and need some help from you?

Whenever parents are afraid to stand up to the group, and when they worry about their child's being accepted, and when they don't communicate a sense of their personal values or their moral code to their children, their children are more likely to turn to the peer group. Then they will adopt whatever values this group has. It is for this reason that groups that are antisocial, drug-taking, or even bizarre are just as attractive to a searching adolescent as more socially benign and acceptable groups.

Henry's parents should have watched that. When he didn't make it with his old friends, he turned to school dropouts and drug-takers. The only thing they had in common was drug-taking; the only thing they did together was to turn on, at which point they just sat together and were in separate smoke-filled dreams.

SEX

One way the group of peers is really helpful for adolescents is in learning about sex. Your adolescent doesn't necessarily know what sex is all about just because you've always been open with him, answered his questions, and given him some good books to read or sex education classes.

It's a funny thing but most adults think that an adolescent thinks about sex all the time. And adults think that this is a lot of fun. Most adolescents, when they think of their parents, think they know nothing about sex—that at the most their parents had sex as many times as they had children, and anyway, their parents never had *fun* with sex.

Now, if you're a parent, you have one advantage over your child. You know what happens when you're an adult and when you're an adolescent; you've been both. Most of the time, however, by the time you're an adult you want to forget about that early time, because it was so painful.

You see, no book really tells you how funny your body will feel, nor does any help you know that you will think about sex so much. Though you may know what intercourse is, how do you do it?

If you have a group of friends, or even one friend with whom you can talk, you find out that others have the same feelings and that others masturbate too. Of course, you get some funny ideas in the process, but in the long run you find out what it's all about.

When adolescents can have group activities, and group dating, they don't feel so alone and don't have to be so afraid. They can have a girlfriend or boyfriend within the group, but they don't have to get too intense or too close. Of course, they will sound intense about the current relationship to you. But if you think of the series of "crushes," sometimes at the beginning on unobtainable people like movie stars, rock singers, and even teachers, and how they rotate their "steady" dating, you can see that they are diluting the intensity of the sexual situation. Even the famous "telephonitis" keeps a safe distance between them.

This is not to say that adolescents never become involved in sexual relations. But more young adolescents wait until they feel more secure about themselves than anyone knows, because the way things are it has almost become a sin to be a virgin, male or female, once you hit adolescence. And young people are insecure enough, without admitting that failure.

The drug-user is a sexual failure. More often than not, he takes drugs to mask his feelings of sexual inadequacy.

James, age sixteen, was a chronic marijuana smoker. Every other word he used was *fuck*—fuck this, fuck that, it's a fucking shame. James had a girl friend, another smoker. His idea of a good time was to get into bed with her and smoke marijuana. Once he really did try to fuck, but he never made it. However, he fantasized that he was in love and talked about getting his own apartment and setting up a relationship with his girl. This fourteen-year-old girl, who was failing in school because she never did her homework, he dreamed would cook, clean, and—in fact, do all the things for him that his mother did.

Nancy was fourteen when she first got started on drugs. She started because she was unhappy at home, poor in school, and generally not interested in anything. She liked going out with boys because they gave her things, and she also liked being petted. She didn't like sex so much, but she went along. The boys with whom

she became involved were usually older and always
heavy drug-users. By the time she was sixteen, she had
had one abortion, without her parents' knowing anything. When she wasn't on drugs, or with boys, she spent
her time looking at television. She never did much thinking.

THINKING AND SCHOOLING

The adolescent who does poorly in school may feel
troubled and worried because of these difficulties. But he
may also have difficulty in school because he is troubled.
There are many reasons for learning difficulties in adolescence. Sometimes they are just a continuation from an
earlier time; in other cases, particular worries and fears
may interfere with being able to concentrate in school.

In many ways adolescence is the best time for learning
and studying. This is the time when there is a big spurt
in mental capacity, and it's the time of the formation of
abstract thinking. You must be well aware of this when
you think of some of the increasingly esoteric and philosophical discussions in which your teenager tries to involve you.

Today, however, there is some tendency to devalue the
area of intellectual development. There is so much more
preoccupation with physical and emotional development
(especially the expression of feelings) that some lose
sight of the fact that emotional wellbeing is also dependent upon intellectual satisfaction and the self-esteem
that comes from being able to do a job well.

WORK

The period of adolescence is the time for selection of
and preparation for a vocation. Though youngsters
usually think about many interests and need time before
they finally make up their minds, they must at least de-

cide whether or not to go to college, and they must pick some areas for concentration.

Preparation for work is very important, because work after all, is a significant part of living. It is no surprise that drug addicts are particularly lacking in any meaningful work history and usually have very little self-esteem as a result. Often the reason they remain in the drug area is that they have no other vocational skills that can offer them the gratification that comes from work.

IDENTITY

Establishing vocational aspirations, reaching sexual maturity, functioning independently, forming relationships with peers, developing a personal value-system— all the products of a working adolescence lead to a sense of self and a personal answer to the question, "Who am I?"

The young adult needs a clear head to begin to perceive himself in relation to past and future, and to conceptualize past and future in a continuum. When he can do that, he will have developed the ability to know, as you know, what will pass and what will change, and to plan for the kind of future he wishes. He should also be able to expedite his planning. He will have learned in the process to put up with his inevitable growing pains. He will have learned about himself; he will have learned to master anxiety and frustration, which teaches that he can survive; he will have learned skills to enable him to further his dreams and to make them reality; he will have a wide view of his world, present and future. But he will only have these things if he has grown up without the distortion of drugs.

Drug-taking is a form of pollution which disturbs the ecology of adolescent growth.

2. What Every Parent Should Know about Drugs

The big question that keeps gnawing at you is, "How can I prevent Johnny from becoming an addict?" Though that's an important question, there are really many other important things before addiction.

It is no wonder, however, you ask this question. There are so many articles and books about drugs and young people, and so much talk about drug addiction and drug addicts, that it must seem as if all adolescents are on the way to becoming addicts!

Not so long ago, you probably never worried about addiction in reference to your own children. You may have believed then that only poor kids became addicts and that they were all delinquents who came from broken homes or who had parents who just weren't around to see how and what their children were doing and didn't care anyway. That's what you may have believed once. Today you are not so sure.

Today the people down the street have a son who is in trouble in school because he is always freaked out on some drug. The people next door have a daughter who had to be sent to live in one of those drug groups because she is an addict. On the next block a fifteen-year-old boy died. Rumor has it that this occurred because of an overdose of heroin. This makes you wonder what is going on with your own children.

You may have once believed that the drug-pusher was a hardened criminal, usually someone from the slums, uneducated and unskilled, who tried to get rich and be successful by selling drugs to the poor and minority youngsters, the black and Puerto Rican kids. You are not as sure of that today.

You know that Johnny's friend Robert has been selling drugs. He has enough money—sometimes you think too much. You know that there is a problem with drugs in your school, and the pusher may be someone who lives in your neighborhood and even someone going to the school. You've read that every college has its wheeler-dealer in drugs. So now you are worried about addiction and how it concerns your child.

All you hear about today is addiction. Formerly, the only time you thought of this was when you read about it in the papers, about some kid who was involved with criminals—no one you would ever get to know. Today, at almost every PTA meeting, the subject of drug use is on the agenda. In addition, there have been special discussion groups for parents, experts have visited the school to educate you about the varieties and kinds of drugs, and drug education for the children in the school is being considered.

After attending these lectures on drug-abuse prevention at your child's school, or listening to the experts on television, or reading magazine articles, you probably think that you have to become an expert about drugs if you are to help your child.

It sometimes sounds as if, to be a good parent, one also has to be a teacher, a doctor, and a psychologist.

One of the things you have surely had at your PTA meetings, at some time or another, was a lecture on the new math so that you could understand enough to help your child with his homework. In fact, didn't you once have a conference about Johnny's schoolwork with his teacher, and didn't she want you to tutor him better? Was it only in math? How about social science, French, and Latin?

How about psychology? Hasn't someone taught you the best way to bring up your children—the way to speak to them to help them express their feelings?

It has come to the point where it is no longer enough to try to be a good mother or father, and a citizen, a worker, a homemaker. You are asked to be knowledgeable in a million and one areas.

This is nonsense.

You have some expertise in relation to your line of work, your hobby, your studies. Everyone has. There are things you may know more about than most people, and things you can make or fix. There are also many things you don't know about. Who knows everything?

You may be a lawyer, a carpenter, a cook, or anything else, but you are also a parent.

The best expertise for you, as a parent, should be in relation to your own children. You need to know them.

There is nothing you need to know about drugs except that they can be dangerous for your children.

All the knowledge in the world about chemical substances will not help you help your children. There is no proof that a parent must have scientific knowledge about drugs and their use. There is no proof that any parent must be a chemist.

There is also no proof that this kind of knowledge helps children to help themselves so that they don't use or want drugs.

WHY ALL THIS HULLABALLOO ABOUT DRUGS TODAY

Every day more and more people are using more and more drugs. This includes the middle-aged and the old, as well as the young. A good deal of this drug use is socially acceptable, legal, and medically prescribed.

The fact is that, in one way or another, everyone is a drug-user. Most commercially available foods have some kind of chemical additives, either for flavor or preservation, or through crop-growing or animal feeding. This is one kind of problem with many physical and genetic implications and many involuntary victims.

Drug use for mind-altering purposes is another matter. This kind of drug use is within the control of the individual user and is not unique to present times. Throughout history, a wide variety of drugs has been used by different social and cultural groups for many purposes: social, philosophical, religious, and medical. These drugs have been made from herbs and other natural plants, yesterday as well as today. With today's acceleration of knowledge and chemical skills, there are many more man-made substances and increasingly many more man-made problems.

Within recent years there has been a great increase in drug use—to the point of abuse. One has only to clock television advertisements to see the prevalence of drug advertisements. There are all sorts of panaceas for all kinds of ailments, from scaly toes to burping stomachs to jangled nerves—because the magic of today is the magic of chemicals, some commonly known as medicine.

What has upset everyone is how avidly and how frequently young people are turning to the magic of drugs. But why should anyone be surprised? Considering the wide use of many drugs, it is perfectly understandable that young people, who don't have much experience with anything, should look for magic, too. When they feel troubled, because of their own feelings of weakness or because they are dissatisfied and disillusioned with the way things are, why shouldn't they, too, look for magic?

Drugs, in one form or another, are easily available. There are also many very respectable and well-reputed adults who suggest drug use is a solution to problems of the world. What is bothering everyone, though, is how many young people are becoming addicted to the magic of drugs.

WHO BECOMES AN ADDICT

Different kinds of people have become addicts at different times and different places. Addicts have never been limited to the young and poor and delinquent.

There was a time when many people in the United States were addicted to patent medicines, because these medicines contained opium or its derivatives. They became involuntary addicts: They used legally sold and advertised drugs with no idea of the consequences, no intention of becoming dependent upon drugs. These people never thought about the possibility of addiction. Most of them were older people, legitimately seeking relief from pain. Eventually there was some recognition of the problem, as a result of which narcotics were brought under federal control. This greatly reduced the number of innocent people addicted to drugs.

Though doctors were still able to prescribe opiates and some narcotics for medicinal purposes, most of them were careful because they were aware of the danger of addiction. Unfortunately, all doctors were not careful, even as some doctors today. Involuntary addiction is still a problem.

Part of the difficulty lies in the time it takes before anyone realizes what is addictive. This has happened often, when a new wonder-drug is used as a substitute for another addictive drug, only to discover that the new magic contains the old addiction.

When it was discovered morphine was addictive, heroin became the magic substitute. When heroin was discovered to be addictive, the new magic was methadone.

What will be the substitute for methadone? We all know now that methadone, too, is addictive.

There are still many involuntary addicts, due to medical prescriptions for amphetamines, barbiturates, and methadone.

What you are concerned about, however, is what makes someone, particularly a young person, a "voluntary" addict, and you also want to know how to stop him.

There is no such thing as a voluntary addict. There are only people who believe it will never happen to them, and these are people with addiction vulnerability. The younger the drug-user, the greater the probability of his being vulnerable, and the greater his belief will be that he will never become an addict.

Young people try drugs for a variety of reasons. For some it is curiosity. After all, when one is young, the more there is an uproar about something, the more it is forbidden, the greater attraction it may have. There is a great deal of peer pressure in some quarters for the use of drugs in a social manner. This is one factor in trying drugs. Some young people try drugs because they are looking for new experiences, some because they want freedom, some for liberation of sensation, or for change. Some try drugs just for fun. Basically, anyone who uses drugs is looking for some physical, psychological, or social change.

All drug use doesn't result in addiction. How often and how much drug use is continued depends upon the degree to which the drug is believed to achieve the intended result. It also depends upon the personality of the user—whether he has addiction vulnerability. It also depends upon the availability of addictive substances.

A person with addiction vulnerability has one important characteristic: He believes that change can come about by some miracle, something outside of himself. There are many young people who experiment with drugs in an attempt to "get into their heads." They soon find out that using drugs is a less satisfactory way than really getting there by themselves. Generally, these young people have enough resources within their personalities that they don't need miracles. Though they may experiment with drugs, they will not stay with them. Inevitably, they discover that what they want—depth of experience, lasting insights, and mastery of life —doesn't come about that way, even though there may be moments when drugs seem to provide just these things. In the long run, these young people learn that drug use is not meaningful for them.

It is understandable that an adolescent experiments with new things and new ways of living. Such experimentation is necessary to learn new roles for his new becoming-adult self. Because of these new roles and the new demands made upon him by others, as well as his own expectations for himself, anxiety and tension are common. In addition, some of his expectations are very unrealistic and frightening because of his lack of knowledge and experience. Nevertheless, the adolescent who has been relatively successful in earlier life, and who has learned to deal with anxiety and frustration before, will usually learn how to manage these new worries. If, in addition, he has the support of interested parents, he has a lot of help. Usually his experimentation will be circumscribed by the wish to harm neither himself or others. But even he is in danger.

The young person who has not learned to tolerate frustration, tension, and delay in the process of getting what he wants is vulnerable to addiction. He will use drugs instead of learning how to be successful. He will make believe he is achieving his purpose. For another characteristic of the addiction-vulnerable personality is a tendency to deny what is and to believe that what he fantasizes is so.

For example, Bill, a seventeen-year-old who had dropped out of school in his senior year because of truancy and failure, who had been arrested because of involvement in a knife fight, who pushed drugs, described himself as an average, middle-class, white American boy! He considered himself an intellectual, a progressive, and spoke disparagingly of the dull stuck-in-a-rut friends he once had who spent all their time on homework or in athletic pursuits. When confronted with school failure, it was the teachers' fault; with the knife fight, it was the other boys; with drug-pushing, it was a way to make a buck—even though he had well-educated, financially secure parents and a more than adequate allowance. All of these difficulties were seen as coming from outside himself. He had been smoking marijuana regularly since age fourteen. He had used LSD, speed, barbiturates, and heroin. He claimed he could stop whenever he wished. He denied he was an addict.

Bill's lifestyle and history showed that he was always dependent on others, had always been fearful and anxious. In adolescence he attempted to mask these characteristics with bravado. He had been querulous and demanding since infancy, and at seventeen he was not prepared to cope with the strains inherent in growing up. Instead he substituted an ersatz sophistication, bolstered it with drugs, and denied he had any problems. His was a troubled personality. He was addiction-vulnerable, and he needed only the availability of drugs to succumb. He was a middle-class addict. He had never known discrimination; he had never known hunger; he had never lived in a slum. His family was intact; his parents, educated and affluent.

Usually the child who becomes an addict in adolescence tends to be one who has had social, intellectual, and personality problems in his younger years. He enters adolescence without sufficient strength to deal with the problems of growing up. In addition, where there are family problems, where discipline is lax, where parents are uninvolved, too busy, or confused about what to do with him, he will have more difficulty. When drugs are available as they are today, his addiction potential is increased. If these substances are not permitted and not available to him, his difficulties will not be compounded by addiction. There have always been troubled children and troubled adolescents, but the recent proliferation of drugs, the increase in their availability, and the glorification of drug-induced states, have complicated their problems.

Moreover, the modern-day problem of drug abuse has other hazards besides addiction. The use of certain drugs, such as LSD, speed, glue sniffing and barbiturates has dangerous and often fatal consequences for the user. Frequent use of most drugs may change body chemistry. Even onetime use of certain drugs may have strong effects on mind and body. The problem then is not who becomes the addict, but what can become of the adolescent who experiments with drugs.

BEFORE ADDICTION

No one becomes addicted overnight. There is a period before addiction which includes the development of tolerance, the possibility of habituation, and the growth of drug-dependence.

Habituation means that the individual has a desire to keep using a particular drug, usually due to emotional reasons. The user thinks he feels better with it. With some drugs, the addictive drugs, the more they are used the more is needed to produce the effect for which they were originally taken. In effect, the body builds up a tolerance to the drug, and nothing happens unless the dosage is increased. This commonly occurs with the use of alcohol. After a while, the habitual drinker finds that one martini is not enough to get and keep the desired rosy glow. If the alcohol-induced pleasure becomes necessary for a person to keep going, or if he believes it is, he may become dependent upon alcohol. This is also true for many other drugs. In effect, drug-dependence implies a state of psychological or physical reliance upon a particular drug. Such dependence usually results from chronic, periodic, and continued use, as well as the physical and psychological nature of the individual; not everyone who uses a chemical that has mind-altering effects becomes dependent upon it and all martini drinkers don't become alcoholics.

Alcohol is commonly used in a variety of social occasions, and many people can take it or leave it. Many others must have their drink, and at many other times, too. This inability to do without alcohol can lead to alcoholism, or an addiction to alcohol. This applies to other drugs, too.

Addiction comes about when a person has an overwhelming desire to use an addictive drug, an inability to do without it, and regular use to the extent of intoxication. In effect, physical and psychological dependence go hand in hand in reference to addiction.

True addiction is difficult to determine. It frequently becomes obvious only when there is an abrupt stopping in the use of the addictive drug. Then withdrawal symptoms occur. These tend to be uncomfortable, sometimes painful feelings, both physical and psychological. They vary according to the particular drug.

Although heroin and opium are the drugs most commonly thought of as addictive, barbiturates, certain tranquilizers, stimulants in large doses, and alcohol also fall into this area. Alcoholism is the number-one drug problem in the United States, where there are approximately 9 million alcoholics. When their families are considered, it is believed that over 25 million people are affected by alcoholism. This problem also ranks third in causes of death within the United States.

The problem of alcoholism extends over many age groups. It has been and continues to be a serious source of difficulty for a large segment of the population, cutting across all socioeconomic classes. The middle-aged tend to be the greatest abusers, primarily because it takes years to build up tolerance and to cross the line into addiction. However, alcoholism is still the most common addiction. Roughly one out of every ten or twelve people who drink have reached this point, but only after years of heavy drinking. A suggested reason for this greater addiction to alcohol is considered alcohol's availability, relatively low cost, and social acceptability. This is one of the questions under debate in discussions of legalization of a variety of drugs.

The greater concern with drug use by young people as compared to alcohol use may be partly related to concern with the antisocial and delinquent behavior attribtued to addicts and their need to obtain money in illegal ways for drug use. The drug addict is usually unable to work and to keep employment. In addition, drugs are expensive. Though alcohol is readily accessible and cheap by comparison to drugs, the truth of the matter is that alcoholism presents a far more serious problem both in the immediate present and in its implications for the future.

The young person who is habitually drunk, in addition to running the risk of alcohol addiction, is also altering his mind, affecting his body, and escaping from necessary tasks. Alcohol is abused by young people far more often than drugs and in many more respectable homes. Because it lacks the opprobrium of drugs, its danger, particularly for young people, is not sufficiently understood. We are concerned with the degree to which a youngster will be unable to cope with the distortions and effects of alcohol. For example, driving when drunk is a serious hazard for self and others. It has been stated that 50 percent of all the automobile accidents in the United States are caused by drunken drivers. These include the full age range of the population, but it is more dangerous for the younger person, who normally takes more risks and is less cautious.

One of the difficulties with youthful drinking is the fact that too often it is combined with drug-taking for a greater thrill or more intense experience. This is of immediate danger in terms of possible death and serious physical complications of long duration. A new trend is the use of alcohol by many addicts, either with or instead of drugs, even those in so-called withdrawal programs. The combination of alcohol and youth is as serious as drugs and youth.

Amphetamines compose another class of drugs with addictive dangers. This class includes stimulants used to increase alertness, reduce hunger to help in dieting, or induce a feeling of well-being. They are commonly known as B's, uppers, and pep pills, and include Benzedrine and Dexedrine. They are medically prescribed for suppression of appetite; reduction of fatigue or depression; and narcolepsy, a rare illness marked by sudden attacks of sleep; and hyperkinesis, which produces restlessness, disturbance, anger, and agitation in children. Due to mounting evidence that these drugs are minimally effective and potentially dangerous, governmental action to control and limit their use has been taken.

A study of college students indicated that almost one-third of them used amphetamines and that they used this drug more than marijuana.

Although stimulants combat fatigue, they also cause hyperactivity leading to physical abuse of the body, which no longer knows when it is time to stop. Loss of appetite can cause malnutrition. In large doses amphetamines cause agitation, blackouts, and aggressive and violent behavior. Some drug-users even inject speed, and contaminated syringes and needles result in hepatitis and blood infections. Syphilis can be transmitted by the practice of multiperson use of one syringe. These diseases also result from heroin injections.

Hepatitis in a young person is therefore very suspect today, although of course there are other ways in which this illness may be contracted. The dilemma for you is that some doctors will attempt to protect your child by withholding from you the knowledge that the illness occurred because of drug injection. They themselves will know because they can see the needle marks, skin discolorations, and abscesses in arms and legs—all the marks of the drug-shooter.

In addition to ups, there are downs, also called "goofballs" and "sleepers." These are barbiturates and sedatives used to induce sleep and reduce tension and anxiety. This is another serious addictive problem of the general population. To magnify the effects, barbiturates and alcohol are sometimes taken together, a practice that can cause unconsciousness or death. A dose of barbiturates that is less than lethal alone may be fatal when taken in combination with alcohol.

Hallucinogens—psychedelics, psychotomimetics, LSD —are able totally to change perceptions. They can affect feeling, thinking, emotions, and self-awareness. They alter time and space perception and can induce illusions, hallucinations, and delusions—a range of psychotic reactions.

The "bad trip" causes horror and panic. Because of the strong emotions and the loss of the sense of reality, some users feel they are going crazy; others have such feelings of grandeur that dangerous and careless action may be precipitated; prolonged reactions of anxiety, depression, and even psychotic breaks occur. Even infrequent users of LSD have experienced a flashback, sometimes months after the drug was taken. In the flashback many features of the LSD state reoccurs. Sometimes the flashback is caused by physical and psychological stress as well as by drugs, including marijuana. The terror may be overwhelming enough to cause suicide attempts, at which some individuals succeed.

Glue-sniffing is a horror because it has been most common among younger adolescents and children. They use the airplane glue from their hobby of model-building. From this start some go on to volatile hydrocarbons, dry-cleaning fluids, and paint-thinners. Though the effects vary considerably, they are all very dangerous to the body. They also cause dizziness, headaches, and vomiting.

When people worry about drug use, they worry about heroin. Where does it fit into this picture? Heroin accounts for 90 percent of narcotic addiction, but it isn't necessarily the worst form. The problem lies in its association with crime and the poor. This kind of addiction was never, until recently, associated with middle-class users.

"Horse," "junk," "snort," "smack"—they all mean heroin. It is a grayish-white or brownish-white powder, usually sold in small cellophane or plastic bags. It may be sniffed ("snorting"), injected under the skin ("skin-popping"), or injected into a vein ("mainlining").

Besides the danger of blood infections, hepatitis, and abscesses as the result of injections, and the transmission of many diseases, heroin is a highly addictive drug to which tolerance is rapidly developed. Heroin can kill, and the chance of an overdose is very possible. The user has no way of knowing the strength of the dose he is taking; he never knows how much pure heroin is really contained in one bag. Sellers frequently vary the strength of the heroin by cutting it with a variety of additives. Thus, every time someone uses heroin he is risking his life, not only because of the varying heroin content, but because the materials mixed with the heroin may be even more dangerous in themselves. An overdose can cause deep sleep, coma, or an even more serious effect upon the respiratory system: The breathing rate is reduced, as a result of which the supply of oxygen to the body is decreased. Death can follow from the resultant oxygen starvation of the brain. Symptoms of acute heroin poisoning are deep sleep or coma; cold, clammy, or bluish skin; and small, open-pinpoint pupils.

Marijuana is the most controversial of drugs. More books have been written, pro and con, calling marijuana dangerous, harmless, no worse than alcohol and certainly not leading to the same hangovers, nonaddictive, and every other possibility. There are studies claiming it causes brain damage, personality change, and mental illness; other studies say it does none of these things.

Many addicts have smoked marijuana before they moved on to other drugs; in the middle-class addict this is not an uncommon pattern. All marijuana smokers do not become addicts, nor do they necessarily move on to other drugs.

Different marijuana users have different reactions. Some feel that they think and act better than ever before, that they and everyone else are more loving. Some users become suspicious, even paranoid; some feel overwhelmed, lost, and unable to distinguish themselves from their surroundings. Some feel irritable, some euphoric or drowsy; some feel nothing at all. These differences are caused by the differences between people and also the differences in the same drug over time. There is great variability because of different body chemistries, users' expectations, places and means of taking any particular drug, and potencies of the drugs themselves. Because drugs are illegal and must be obtained through criminals, the contents of a drug is always uncertain.

Mind-altering substances also have different effects upon different people because they have different personalities; even the same person cannot be absolutely sure what to anticipate each time because of variations in emotional feeling and physical state. As a result, each drug experience is a gamble.

Another problem has to do with the increasingly common practice of multidrug use. Youngsters have been known to raid the medicine cabinet and indiscriminately take whatever drugs may be there. It has been reported that in some communities, children as young as eleven years of age have collected pills from the medicine cabinet and brought them to pajama parties. There the group pooled its pills and divided them—one yellow, one blue, one green. We have talked with youngsters whose first drug experiences were with grandma's digitalis pills, or mother's diet pills, that they found in the medicine cabinet. Their explanations for taking these seemed to be related to their wishes for escape from a current situation, or just for kicks.

In the long run the biggest problem is not addiction. The biggest problem is before addiction: the use of drugs that may be dangerous for anybody, and that are more dangerous for growing bodies and minds. The problem is the dangers to which your child may be exposed.

WHAT YOU REALLY NEED TO KNOW

Once you know that drugs can be dangerous for your child, you probably want to know how you can tell if he is using them and what you can do to stop him.

There is no one who should know better than you if there is something wrong and if your child is using drugs, if you are not afraid to know. You need to be as knowledgeable about your own children as possible and unafraid to face the fact that your child may be in trouble and may be using drugs. Of course if you question any behavior that disturbs you, it is not uncommon for children to deny the facts or make up some cock-and-bull story.

Sally was a fifteen-year-old girl who was not attending school. Her schoolwork became poor. Suddenly she had different friends and was taking part in different activities. She had been an active child; now she became sullen and withdrawn. Her parents were angry with her, and there were a lot of fights. One of the things that worried them was that she was always hanging out in a pizza store. Her father even yelled at her that everybody in the neighborhood knew this was a place where junkies congregated.

However, they didn't do anything but yell. They didn't investigate the store or the possibility that Sally used drugs, nor did they discipline her. They never really found out how she was spending her time—almost as if they were afraid to know. The consequences were inevitable. Two years later they learned that Sally was an habitual heroin-user, and that this had been preceded by frequent use of a wide variety of drugs. They never knew what to do. Because of that feeling of helplessness, they did nothing.

Marvin's parents didn't like the way he locked himself in his room, day after day, nor did they like the pungent odors that they smelled coming from there. When they confronted him with using marijuana, he admitted this was so, but said marijuana helped him think and there was nothing wrong. They protested that they didn't like him to use drugs. Marvin said marijuana was less harmful than the alcohol they themselves used, and anyway, they didn't know anything about marijuana because they hadn't tried it.

They agreed; they knew nothing about marijuana. However, they knew he was too young for drugs—alcohol, marijuana, or any other kind of drug. Furthermore, they knew him and they knew that coming home from school day after day and locking himself in was just not like him, and they wanted to know what was wrong.

Marvin started to cry. He was having trouble with his French teacher, who was always making fun of him. Marvin was finding it very hard to learn a new language, and he made a lot of mistakes when he was called upon. The teacher would mimic him, and the whole class would laugh at him. But the teacher did more than that. Since Marvin was fat, the teacher would call on Marvin and ask him in French, "Do you like to eat?" or "What did you have for dinner?" Marvin would have to reply in French—and the whole class would laugh.

The parents agreed this was embarrassing. They helped him in two ways. First, they immediately discussed this problem with the French teacher and the guidance teacher. The French teacher had thought it would help Marvin to become aware of his obesity. Second, they decided with Marvin that if weight was a problem, they would help him with it. The family menus were changed, and an exercise regime was established for him.

All of this was more helpful than the make-believe induced by marijuana. This is the kind of help you need to be able to give your child. To help in this manner, you need to know him and know how you feel about his current behavior.

You know that when he was little, the best barometer of his illness was your awareness that something was wrong. At times you were able to sense he had a fever just from looking at him and noticing that he looked different and acted different. You knew this even before you used the thermometer. It isn't that much different now that he is older. If you notice an unexplainable change in your adolescent's behavior, you need to consider drug use as one of the possible reasons.

Knowledge about specific drugs will not help you, because so many of their symptoms may also reflect other causes. If you become a drug expert, and only that, you may sometimes accuse him of doing something he hasn't yet thought of doing. If you ignore the possibility of drug use, you will let him down. Very often young people use drugs because they feel troubled and hope to get some attention in that way.

George, a fourteen-year-old boy whose parents had recently divorced felt very unhappy about the disintegration of his family life. Although he lived with his mother, he was not sure of her interest or affection. He would go to school on downs and be sent to the school nurse whenever the teacher became alarmed by his drowsiness and sluggish behavior. Then the nurse would call his mother to come and take him home. Finally, on one occasion George became acutely hysterical from taking ups. His mother became frightened, called her ex-husband, and then called a therapist, who advised that George be taken to a hospital. There he was sedated. In this instance the extreme use of different drugs served to bring his parents' attention to a child in an unhappy home situation. Later George admitted that he took drugs to get to a therapist whom he wished would see his parents in the hope that his home situation could be improved. He thought that drug use was the only method drastic enough to get his parents interested in him. Perhaps if he had talked to a school guidance counselor, school nurse, or some interested adult, he could have received some help. But he did not try to deal with his fears. Instead, he used the availability of dangerous drugs to get temporary attention and relief from his feelings of being unloved.

The knowledge you need, therefore, is knowledge about your child. If it seems to you that your youngster suddenly appears very glum and depressed, when he had been more or less pleasant before, you surely don't need some expert to tell you that something is wrong. Similarly, if he seems to be falling asleep at inappropriate hours, appears agitated and restless, looks flushed, with glassy eyes and slurred speech, looks rundown and has lost weight, or appears nervous, you surely will become concerned. No doubt you realize that any one of these symptoms may be explained by a variety of causes.

Sometimes, if no action occurs early enough, the troubled behavior increases beyond physical and emotional disturbances, and social and academic activities suffer. School grades may go down, social activities may change markedly, your child may need more money than usual, or he may suddenly have more money. If, for whatever reason, you did not notice changes in his behavior when he began to use drugs, you may see them when he tries to stop. For example, the chronic heroin-user appears to be functioning well when he has enough of the drug for his addiction, but he will appear abnormal when he stops using the drug. Then he will seem hyperactive, agitated, and restless, and be unable to sleep. On the other hand, the chronic amphetamine-user will appear depressed and lethargic when he is not abusing amphetamines.

Some say that the immediate physical effects of smoking marijuana cigarettes will sometimes be red eyes, and a cough, because of the irritating effect of the smoke on the lungs. Marijuana-users are supposed to get very hungry about one-half to one hour after smoking. However, anyone who has ever observed the eating habits of adolescents, their unpredictable and frequently voracious need for food, will know what a problem this is for a parent turned drug-detective.

Even the smell of marijuana creates a dilemma. When it is smoked, it releases a pungent, aromatic odor which is not unpleasant. Some novices think it smells like incense. Today incense-burning and scented candles are fashionable, though, and both may be used to hide the odor of marijuana. They may also be used because of association with the mystical East, with romance and mystery.

Some marijuana-users become irritable, suspicious, and anxious. Others feel euphoric or drowsy, and show a tendency to withdraw into themselves. You see how the problem is compounded: The first probably sounds like a description of your son Tuesday, and the last as he was Wednesday. By Thursday the picture was completely different.

Knowing your own child in relation to how he has been and how he is, is more helpful in the long run than anything you can learn about drugs. Knowing yourself and what makes you anxious, and facing up to it, is helpful too. After all, sometimes parents worry too much, and just as often this is as bad as not worrying enough.

Knowing what to do about all of this is more difficult. Obviously the first thing is to see how you can correct conditions for your child within the home and his immediate environment. Sometimes this will mean changes for you as well as for him. You may need the advice of someone else, and this may be difficult for you too.

It is not easy to know what to do. That's part of the dilemma in which you find yourself.

3. The Parental Dilemma or Let's Speak for Parents

Some people say that the twentieth century didn't really begin until the bomb was dropped on Hiroshima. If that is so, you, as a parent, are probably a product of the nineteenth century, with out-of-date mores and values. At least that is what your children and many other people are probably telling you, in one way or another.

Maybe you think of your self as enlightened. Maybe you try very hard at least to know the issues and values about which your kids rap. But probably even you are dismayed by how difficult it is to bridge the generation gap. When you try to express understanding and try to find some ground for agreement, more often than not you are met with the response, "You don't understand at all." Not only that—sometimes it seems as if your children don't really want you to understand them; they will do nothing to help bridge the gap.

What does it feel like to be the parent of an adolescent today? How is it as you struggle to help your children grow in a world so different from that in which you grew —a world whose technology so threatens all to the point where virtually nothing is predictable and living with uncertainty becomes the primary challenge? What do you think of when you realize that a significant problem to be faced in relation to your child is the threat of drug abuse?

A minimum response would be the experiencing of unusual anxiety and tension. In the face of the current so-

cial scene, because of what adolescence is said to be today, because of the gap in communication that may exist
between you and your child, and because of the experts
and their advice—it would not be surprising if you have
almost given up your right to decide anything more for
your children.

You are finding little support for your responsibilities
in our society, which often seems instead to undercut
your authority. But when your adolescent's behavior is
not sufficiently conforming in social institutions, you are
the primary recipient of blame.

On the one hand, the "reactionary," "dictatorial" parent is denigrated, and the total individual, group per-
missiveness, and desirability of experimentation—with
sex, drugs, and education—are preached as necessary for
your child. On the other hand, the lack of parental authority and the predicted disintegration of the family are
viewed by many as precursors to disaster and the reasons for adolescent difficulty. Clearly confusion
abounds!

If you are an average parent you wish to see your children grow and prosper, and you attempt to support those
behavior patterns and experiences that you believe will
enhance their development. You have aspirations for
your children's achievement, and you work hard to get
the means to help them get somewhere—somewhere that
is generally socially acceptable. You may have differing
degrees of flexibility in dealing with the changing behavior of your adolescent. On your community, its size and
economic situation, will depend what you will worry
about and even what kind of help will be available to
you.

The confusion, frustration, anger, and helplessness of
many of you in relation to your dilemma about what to
do and what kind of parent to be, have too often resulted
in an increased yielding of your rights and your responsibility to take stands, have expectations, and set limits.

You have the right to be an "old-fashioned parent."
That's what all good parents eventually end up being.
The dilemma is that today, more than any other time,
being old-fashioned is unpopular.

THE GENERATION GAP

Your confusion is deepened by the memory of your own
adolescence. Then it was viewed by your parents and society as a short transitional phase between childhood
and adulthood. In fact, there wasn't so much talk then
about adolescence and adolescent problems. Some esca-
pades were expected, but serious problems happened
only in somebody else's home. The entire family did not
have to change because of changes in the adolescent.
Marriage and the beginning of a new family were on the
horizon. Within less than half your lifetime, however,
adolescence has emerged as a major life-stage, resulting
in the reorganization of school systems to provide the
special milieu deemed necessary because of the special
needs and problems of this age group. In addition, a
whole series of specialized physical and psychological
services have also developed.

If your children are in high school, in theory at least
they are considered well on their way to being grownup,
even if they are only fourteen or fifteen. At least that's
what they keep telling you. You probably feel, based on
your life experience, that it really will not be very long
before they will be faced with big decisions about work,
marriage, and a family, for all which you feel they are
still so ill-prepared. It is so difficult to know what is going on inside them, because they don't seem to want to
tell you. And even worse, when they are not in school,
some of them find every excuse to be away from home
with their friends, many of whom you don't even know.
If you want to know, you may be told that you can't let
go. After all, Bob's mother and father don't ask all those
questions.

Also, their mood swings are so unfathomable. Just at the moment that you may feel that you are making some headway in being able to talk together, you are suddenly closed off by a wall of silence or an angry outburst. When they are at home, what you perceive as simple, reasonable expectations, such as taking care of their rooms or lending a hand with the chores, may be experienced by your adolescent children as monumental demands. You are probably shocked by behavior that you don't recall as part of your experience at that age. You wouldn't have dared.

Actually, this is not exactly true. If you think back, you will probably remember one of your parents exclaiming, "I don't know what this new generation is coming to!" Your grandmother probably said this in her time, too.

A conflict between generations has always been a normal part of life. It comes about because of the necessary changes in adolescence to a new self in a different world than the parents knew. The world has always changed from one generation to another, even if at some times and places the changes appear slower and more gradual—usually only in historical perspective.

Peter Blos, an analyst of the phenomenon of adolescence, suggests that the notion of "generation gap" is a device used to create so vast a distance between young and old, that they become incapable of meeting in either mind or body. As a consequence the conflict between generations that is essential for growth both of self and of civilization is avoided.

Disagreements between you and your child will not hurt him. They are inevitable and in the long run help him define the differences between you and himself, one of the very important tasks of his adolescence. As he works through these areas of conflict with you and with other representatives of the older generation in the larger society, he helps to define himself, his values, and needed changes in the larger world. He can refine his ideals and develop his philosophy.

If there is no conflict, if you understand everything, accept and agree with all he does, you leave little for him to learn to understand by himself. His identity loses its clarity and its strength.

The dilemma of the generation gap is not yours alone; the glorification of the youth culture is part of today's scene and involves the total society.

THE EXPERTS

The experts in education, the social sciences, and the "helping" professions do their bit to widen the gap. It seems that often in their struggle to both understand and provide adequate social arrangements for helping young people to grow, they tend to undermine the appropriate role of parents. They neglect to use their combined resources of values and knowledge to encourage connectedness between parents and their adolescent children. Too frequently there is failure to question who has expertise for what and to acknowledge the incompleteness of what is available in the realm of fact. More often than not, the focus is on parental weakness, rather than supporting the positive potential of parents who should be encouraged to trust themselves.

What you find in the literature does little to support your image as helper to your children. In addition to reinforcing your sense of hazard, you find spelled out and underscored all of the potentially pathological hurdles *you* present to your children, or scientific instructions that thoroughly negate either your individual needs and problems or those of your children. Unfortunately, so much of the literature is focused on psychopathology, and so little recognizes that you also have the capacity to master the challenges presented by your children's growth.

To expand on your very real dilemma, you need only a cursory review of the mass media—television, popular magazines, and the press—and the professional literature of psychiatrists, psychologists, social workers, other mental health personnel, and educators. All dramatically define adolescence as a developmental phase fraught with danger. The emphasis is on the high potential for psychological maladjustment and destructive social behavior.

In essence, though the tasks of separation and individuation from the family are critical in the process of becoming an adolescent and moving to adulthood, this process must be differentiated from alienation. The process of individuation necessarily includes both you and your youngsters as the actors. Alienation involves the withdrawal of essential emotional caring and trying. Talk of alienated young people concerns their resignation and hopelessness. Alienation that involves parents themselves appears to be a reaction to the separation and individuation process of their children, when the parents have given up all hope for communication and when connectedness has broken down.

Too many of you today anticipate your children's adolescence with apprehension. You do not have to feel hopeless and helpless. The large majority of our young people work out relationships with adults, perhaps different ones from those of the past or future. But very frequently they incorporate parental values. There are many studies comparing adolescents' beliefs with those of their parents which attest to the similarity in their values, despite highly publicized opinions to the contrary.

A trusting relationship between you and your child is necessary to his learning how to be an adult. Conflict and difference of opinion need not undercut trust. The stereotype of adolescence as a sorely troubled period is interfering too frequently with your expectations that your children will make it. Without talking simplistically about the power of positive thinking, there is much evidence to support the sociological concept of the self-fulfilling prophecy. It stands to reason that an apprehensive climate of expectation increases anxiety and tension. If you are living with such apprehension, you must of necessity struggle with feelings related to flight, or alienation.

Your ability to maintain connectedness in feeling with your children is important in helping adolescents. Sometimes this involves remembering the fears, doubts, and struggles of your own adolescence by way of increasing your understanding of that with which your children are struggling. Meanwhile, you still have to know your present feelings, attitudes, and values, as parent and adult.

For some of you knowing your real feelings and knowing who you are is very difficult. Partly this occurs because of the cultural emphasis on youth which has further worsened your conflict and confusion. Some of you, like all of us today, want so much to be young, and may have worked overtime to demonstrate your ability to diminish generation differences. Not only does this dull who mom and dad are, but it adds to the anxieties of the very youngsters whom you would like to resemble. It is simpler for a young person to deal with prohibitions and taboos than with contradictions, confusion, and inconsistency.

THE NEW EDUCATION

If you are currently finding little support from psychological quarters, you are in even rougher waters on the educational scene. The serious problems of public education, particularly in large urban schools must sorely threaten your aspirations for your children's achievement and wellbeing. You not only have to worry about what your children are learning, you have to worry because the schools also appear unable to protect your children. In too many instances you are finding that they are a malignant social environment and the focus for considerable drug-pushing. You must feel overwhelmed by the inability of the educational authorities to enforce discipline. And what can you do about young teachers who believe there is nothing wrong with drug use such as the smoking of marijuana, and who may make it available to your child?

If you have tried to find out about what is going on in school and with the curriculum, which you may perceive as alien, you may have been met with a series of impressions and responses which increased your discomfort. The discipline and order which were part of your school experience must seem to have given way to a laissez-faire atmosphere where there is much wandering around and boys and girls are all over the place.

In addition, you have usually not taken part in the decision-making about the direction of the curriculum. You may feel that, though you disagree with much that is going on in the school, to disagree may create problems for both yourself and your child. Some of you may have been fortunate to meet with school personnel who made an effort to bring you on board about new curricular trends. These may or may not be consonant with what you think education ought to be.

You have seen the frustration of some of the older teachers who are struggling to shift gears and accommodate to a philosophy of education very different from the way they had been prepared for teaching. Or the teacher may seem very young, bearded, and not as well-put-together as you might like when you think about teachers as adult role-models for your youngsters.

You may have tried to express your reactions to what was going on in the school. In some instances, you may have met with a sympathetic but helpless response; in others, there may have been a tolerant but mildly arrogant unspoken appraisal of your less-than-expert status; in still others, you may have found downright rudeness.

You are confronted, too, by the realization that larger and larger areas of responsibility are now perceived as within the province of the school. Part of the curriculum of many schools includes sex education, drug education, family education, career education, and college selection. Have you ever felt that the only thing left is for you to clean the house, cook the food, do the laundry, and provide the money for everything, including all the educations?

THE SEXUAL DILEMMA

The difference between generations is always heightened in reference to problems of sex. Traditionally the adolescent has greater interest in sex than his parents usually would like. In your adolescence you probably assumed that your parents would disapprove of almost everything you thought and at least half the things you did—which you did anyway.

Today the tables are turned. There appears to be as great concern with the disequilibrium in the lives and emotions of parents because of their adolescents' emerging sexuality, as with the sexuality of the adolescents! It has been suggested that youngsters' sexual interests may activate, in some parents, their own unresolved sexual conflicts. This may heighten competitiveness between parents and child at a time when the parent perceives his own powers are waning. In some instances the situation exacerbates existing sexual problems between husband and wife.

Yes, all this is possible and sometimes occurs. It is true that in some families the disequilibrium created does result in difficulty. Most of you, however, are not so immature that you cannot experience pleasure and satisfaction in seeing your children become adults.

The problem may be that you do not approve of the new sexual freedoms. You have a right to be concerned about the shift in sexual mores. This shift may have a happy potential for the emotional lives of young people, but no one yet knows for sure.

You live with your children and know about the pressure they experience in feeling the need to live up to the expectation of their peers that they experiment even though they may be unready to do so. You probably have strong disapproval of providing the pill to a thirteen-year-old daughter so that she may be free to experience sexuality. You may have strong feelings about homosexuality, because you don't see how it will get your child anywhere, and certainly won't help you complete your lifecycle by becoming a grandparent. You may feel that masturbation is not such a wonderful thing that it has to be glorified and taught, and oral sex, though it may not cause pregnancy, isn't what you hope your child will enjoy. You may believe in romantic love and deplore sleeping around. You may be terribly old-fashioned. But if the experts continue to downgrade parental conservatism in relation to your children's emerging sexuality and exclude recognition of your possible protective role, they will lessen the possibility of your being helpful.

DRUGS

When you come to the drug scene, there is even more of a problem. In many ways your attitude and ability to take a firm stand against drug experimentation may have been weakened by your own use of chemical substances for relief of stress. Consequently, this makes you vulnerable to the arguments of your articulate children who point to your readiness to take a pill or a drink as they seek to rationalize their own drug use. Incidentally, research does suggest that there is an association between parents' use of drugs and the incidence of drug usage among children. Ideally, we all ought to find better ways to handle stress. However, if it is your assessment that drug use in adolescence has dangerous consequences for mastering growth tasks, that you are different from your children, and that age does make a difference, you have a right to be supported in that role. It is no wonder, however, if you are confused in this area, too. The therapeutic community's participation in the dialogue about the pros and cons of drug use, has added to this confusion.

Add to this your awareness of the availability of drugs. Perhaps when you were young and hung around on the corner or at the drugstore, a good deal was being said and done that you wouldn't have wanted your parents to know about. "Dirty" jokes, sexually stimulating talk, and smoking cigarettes surreptitiously were part of the scene, but not drugs. And if you have begun to read more and more in the press and in popular magazines, you know that even in good neighborhoods, drugs are no more than a telephone call away or are even being pushed by your youngster's classmates. If you are really being touched by the antidrug efforts, you may be getting uncomfortable about the sleeping pills your doctor prescribed for you when you have a particularly difficult day and cannot fall asleep, or the Dexedrine that you took the last time you went on a diet. This is a pill-pushing culture and instant solutions are constantly sought. You need to be concerned about what medications are benignly sitting in your medicine chest which unknowingly may be a beginning for experimentation.

To assist your young adolescent children and to prevent their using drugs, you need to take a definite stand on any drug use. Most of you are against the use of alcoholic beverages by youngsters. You really should be just as opposed to all drug use, even marijuana. This is no problem if you are convinced of the dangers of the use of chemicals, particularly by young, growing children. Where your moral and religious beliefs include such prohibitions, these too should be communicated.

The dilemma you are in is caused by the fuzziness of the information available about marijuana. Some say it's not harmful, it is less dangerous than alcohol, or it is not habituating. But it is a chemical, it does alter the mental state, and it won't harm your children only if you insist that young children do not need and should not have any chemically induced euphoria.

If you view your youngster's drug use as a symptom of social disorganization and part of the times, and feel yourself powerless, there is little hope to counteract what appears to be a social trend undermining the family's importance and strength.

THE IMPORTANCE OF THE "OLD-FASHIONED" PARENT

You can be helpful if you have clear rules which you clearly communicate to your children. These should concern his activities at home and at school, curfews, and privileges, and responsibilities. Maybe compromises will be necessary after you talk things over, but they should never be at the expense of your values or when you have real misgivings. If despite this clarity of communication, you become concerned about some behavior, this concern should be aired. This will help you and your child.

The mother of a fifteen-year-old boy told the following story. One evening the father, noticing that his son seemed unusually exhilarated, almost high, questioned his son about his activities. The youngster had been engaged in very exciting and satisfactory dramatic activities and had come home unusually stimulated which he expressed in rather giddy behavior. The father was satisfied with his son's explanation, but the next morning the boy complained to his mother about his father's questioning of him. The mother supported the father's inquiries and clearly stated that her son could expect that both mother and father would hold him accountable for his behavior now, and in the future—because they cared about him. To this, the boy nodded Yes, he knew.

With older children, particularly, there will not be such simple acquiescence. But what is wrong with an open disagreement? At least the air will be cleared. In fact, adolescents will frequently attempt to obtain some parental guidlines in devious ways, even through misbehavior. Even though they often complain about the restrictions, it is quite obvious that they are relieved when some external controls are provided. When these are not available, some adolescents may need to act in an increasingly destructive manner, to themselves through the use of drugs, to others in a variety of social delinquencies, or in both ways, until their cry for help is heard.

This story also illustrates another point, the importance of support and cooperation of one parent by another in disciplinary measures. Of course, there may be differences of opinion between you and your spouse at times, but these need to be worked out between you. Your child must not be permitted to play one against the other. For example, if a father provides a weekly allowance for his son, who feels it is insufficient, and the son then complains to his mother, who supplements the allowance, it would be better if this boy could come to some more satisfactory arrangement through discussion with his father.

It would assist him in his socialization and tolerance of tension, and prepare him for adult responsibilities. If the mother really disagrees with the father, it will help their marriage and their child for them to talk about their differences with each other.

You also need to know about your children's friends and to encourage them to spend time at home, but not without adult supervision and some awareness of your presence and restrictions on activities in the home. Similarly, adolescents should not be allowed to participate in activities in homes where responsible adults are not present. After all, what better place to fool around with drugs than in the safety of one's living room when parents are away!

All of this is very old-fashioned advice. Your children will not like it, but if you help them reflect on some of the things that go on in social gatherings and with some of their friends, and if they are honest with themselves, they will understand. At least, they will be sure that you care for them and are still willing to help them. It will be very reassuring for your child to be secure in this knowledge. It will leave him free to struggle with his own problems of growing up.

You really need to continue to provide protection to your growing children, even though they talk about wanting to be on their own. With all adolescents, and particularly the younger ones, you are the key to providing a climate which will be helpful to them.

To control youthful drug use, you need to be strengthened in your confidence and know-how. Yes, the peer group is an important force, but it is not enough, and not good enough. The peer group frequently has been identified as an important causative factor in a youngster's drug use, but its influence has been found to be minimal unless parents have abdicated their own. Too often this occurs when parents themselves question the potency of family influence and its values.

Despite all the hullaballoo about the death of the family, the family is, and will continue for some time to be, the crucial influence on children's values and behavior. Adolescents still need and want a reasonably reliable and predictable family group in which they can test out their ideas and actions before trying them out in the world. They need a family to which they can return for understanding, guidance, and emotional refueling.

However, it may be possible that, even when you have done all you think proper, problems still persist. Your child may be having difficulty in school, or with friends; there may be problems at home and general unhappiness; you may be worried because you think or know that he is involved with drugs. You might want to look for help outside of the immediate family. Sometimes it is helpful for him to have the opportunity to speak to an adult other than his parent, such as a relative, friend of the family, clergyman, or teacher. Any of these people also may be helpful to you.

If difficulties persist, you may want to consider whether therapy could be of assistance to you and your children.

Part II
All about Therapy

4. The Seduction of the Professional Community

There are few terms as ambiguous as "therapy" and "therapeutic." Their meanings can vary with different tellers and different listeners, and at different places and different times.

Sometimes "therapy" is accompanied by a descriptive adjective: occupational therapy, physical therapy, dance therapy, group therapy, drug therapy. Similarly, "therapeutic" modifies and alters something else: therapeutic milieu, therapeutic community, or therapeutic measure. Therapy generally is assumed to be helpful for someone.

In the sense in which the term is used in this book, it implies a meeting between two participants, each of whom has a different role: One is the helper, the other is being helped. The helper is supposed to have particular knowledge and skill; the helpee, a particular need. Therapy most frequently means that a person with specific training, usually a professional, uses certain methods to assist a person with a need or problem to get better; the training and skill of the therapist is also supposed to be relevant to the problem of the person needing help.

This isn't always so, however, particularly when drug use is involved.

The problem of drug use by young people has seduced everyone, both the politicians and the professionals, including therapists. The politicians have provided the money, and the professionals have set to work on doing something after the problem has taken root; they are all busy doing something *after* addiction.

The drug problem is not properly diagnosed when the emphasis is on addiction; the drug problem in which you are interested is that of helping the kid who uses drugs not to become an addict and that of helping him not to hurt himself. To help him, *his* problems have to be understood.

It is not enough to say that someone is a drug-user. You have to know what it is that troubles him so much that he turns to drugs and help him with *that* problem. When you know that, the relevant skill can be applied to the relevant problem by a person trained in the relevant knowledge.

But understanding the problem of a drug-using adolescent in this way takes time, more time than people seem to wish to spend on adolescents. Time seems in shorter supply than money in the world today. It is almost as if, now that man can travel to the moon and rival the speed of light, he is hooked on speed; he is always demanding instant satisfaction from instant technology.

The professional community is not immune to this speed mania. Much of the therapy it supports involves high-speed, brief approaches; too much of the "therapy" that is available for drug-users is not provided by professionals themselves. The latter have, more often than not, become the supervisors and administrators, and "therapy" is left to ex-drug addicts with minimal—if any —training.

Too often, the type of therapy that you will find for your child will depend upon where you are, who you are, with whom you make contact, and what is available. You should not be so helpless—and you should not be uninformed. After all, before you buy a product, or before you contract for a service, you frequently examine the product, read reports for consumers, and ask many questions.

Therapy is not so sacrosanct that it shouldn't be questioned, too. After all, this concerns the welfare of your child and yourself. You have every right to know the good and the bad—what to look for and what to avoid.

One of the things you should avoid is more drugs, or "drug therapy" for your adolescent child, if you can. Unfortunately, professionals have become drug-pushers more often than you realize.

SEDUCTION BY DRUGS

Some professionals, recognizing the body-damage implications of any drug use, believe it necessary to refer youthful drug-users to a medical facility or drug treatment center, with the thought that medical intervention is needed. Too often this decision is made before the degree of drug use and its reversibility has been determined. Unfortunately, most treatment centers and drug programs make little differentiation between the addict and the user. Frequently, treatment plans are wholesale, unindividualized, and based on the assumption that all drug use equals addiction. Such lack of diagnosis is destructive to the effort to help the adolescent *before* he is an addict.

Drug treatment in some medical setting may even be dangerous. Referral to medical auspices has sometimes resulted in a careless dosage of drugs, such as methadone, that may kill and most certainly is addictive. Too often a prescription is given without adequate knowledge of the individual's previous drug use and without careful study of the possibility of rehabilitation without the guaranteed addiction to methadone. Many an adolescent has been turned on to the too easily obtainable peace of methadone by socially acceptable, respectable sources.

Joseph, a seventeen-year-old boy, who was snorting three bags of heroin a week, wanted to kick the habit. This is a minimal amount, indicating that he had some control and was not yet addicted. However, he did not want to undergo the struggle and frustration of stopping without chemical assistance. When he reported to a privately run methadone center, the only personnel he saw was an ex-addict. Joseph was informed that his heroin use would not qualify him for methadone. As a "favor," his heroin use was put down on the chart as nine bags per week! He was given the corresponding methadone supply. He was not examined by a physician, nor was his age verified, even though it is illegal to provide methadone for a young person under eighteen.

The physician in charge of that clinic was really a pusher, a professional perpetrator of drug abuse.

Another area of inadvertent pushing is illustrated in the April 1970 issue of *Science World,* a scholastic magazine that is sold and distributed in junior high and high Schools. There the ins and outs of ups and downs were carefully explained: what gives relief from pain and anxiety, and what provides a high. Would it be considered educational to describe various forms of sexual deviation in order to provide sex education?

Educational institutions have been affected by the drug seduction in another way. They, too, reflect the belief in the magic of drugs and have resorted, at times, to using drugs as panaceas for problems, to them, of control and discipline. For example, teachers having difficulty in controlling disruptive and very young children have been known to request that their parents obtain medication from the children's physicians. This medication has then been administered to the child in the classroom by the teacher, or by the principal, even though nothing in the training of educators equips them for this task. In the first place, neither the teacher nor the principal has the comprehensive knowledge to assess the reasons for such disruptive behavior. Such knowledge might lead to a different kind of intervention. Secondly, they are not prepared for the responsibility of monitoring the potential adverse reactions of drugs.

The physicians who provide the tranquilizers and amphetamines for "hard-to-manage" children have been criticized in many medical circles for careless, poorly diagnosed treatment that has the potential to addict very young children.

Sometimes an additional problem in helping the drug-using youth involves the helper's lack of emotional objectivity. This may come about because of all the confusion pertaining to the subject of drug use. In addition, there are some who need to find some rationalization to justify and accept drug-using because of their own experimentation with illegal drugs.

You probably know of some people in the professional community who have, in their personal lives, accepted present values and styles even to the extent of using a variety of drugs and of making them available to youngsters. One mother recorded her anguish when during a holiday the family met a young psychiatrist and his wife who generously offered a joint to her sixteen-year-old daughter.

THE SEDUCTION OF YOUTH

You cannot automatically assume that professionals have different value-systems than young people. Some are no less vulnerable to the seduction of the adolescent and his culture than any other segment of this youth-oriented society. Consider the bearded, Levi-clad, bead-wearing psychotherapist or educator who is as frequently seen at national conferences as the similarly garbed adult is on television. When parents express this pervasive need to be youthful, they have been used as the barb of the cartoonists' wit and the advertising man's slogans.

Of course everyone has the right to be stylish and to dress as he or she will. But the extent of the vulnerability to the seduction of trying to remain ever young needs to be understood. The problem is said to be in adult envy of the youthful vigor and the perceived freedom of adolescents. Certainly, parents are frequently accused of this. Why isn't it possible for professionals to be similarly stimulated?

There are those who rationalize their own drug experimentation and their acceptance of drug use by young adolescents as empathic, modern, and aware of the present scene. They do not accept that they have been seduced to abandon their professional responsibilities.

People who work in professional capacities with children and young adolescents have to think of themselves as surrogate guardians for them. In such a role, there is and needs to be a generational distance and a general distance in the service of objectivity.

Certainly you, as the parent, would expect this to occur.

Now empathy is important: It is the ability to understand the experience of another as if one were the other. It does not imply that one must experience *in reality* as the other does. If you consider the wide range of traumatic situations that human beings experience, you can see that it is impossible and, in fact, undesirable for any one individual to experience everything. What is essential is an ability to understand what an experience may have been and how it may have been perceived by another. An objective detachment as well as an objective view of what an adolescent's particular world may really be can enable an empathic knowledge of the adolescent and *his* perception of *his* world. Being in his world, on the contrary, tends to blur distinctions between the helper and the other, and confuses the needs and rights of each.

Historically, adolescents have been expected to talk about wanting freedom and to be critical of society and of the older generation. This may be healthy and necessary for them. Today the adolescent who speaks critically of the conformity and materialism of present-day society may be speaking to a humanistically concerned and reality-oriented professional. However, the latter cannot assume that the criticism means the same to the adolescent as it does to himself. What needs to be understood is the meaning of such criticism to the young person himself. It is more helpful for the young person if *his* opinions are better understood *by himself* so that he may eventually arrive at that satisfied state of knowing who *he* is and where *he* is going. Neither encouragement of revolt nor encouragement of conformity per se is helpful for adolescents.

It can be helpful to remember the needs and feelings of youth and to assist young people to synthesize their past with their present and their anticipated futures through remembering rather than acting. Interested older people who are concerned with the welfare of young people can offer themselves as role-models and can also hold out some hope for making it. They can also make the trying worthwhile.

A problem in many drug programs is the de-emphasis of the importance of adults in the lives of young people and the emphasis upon peers. It is as if the professional community has swallowed hook, line, and sinker the youth culture of today without regard for or consideration of the contribution one age group can and must make to another.

A few years ago a community organization attempted a survey of successful residents of East Harlem. Success was defined as having achieved a better job and a better education than one's parents, a common and very acceptable criterion in our culture. In this group of Puerto

Rican, black, and Italian people, more than half had completed college and one quarter had even higher educational degrees. Their parents had had little education, and all had been very poor. When the individuals involved were asked about the specific difficulties they had encountered in growing up, they mentioned poverty and inadequate schools in their early years. They said that friends in the community who were having fun and avoiding hard work and schooling frequently had made it difficult for them by tempting them to stay away from school. However, almost uniformly, an important element perceived in their achieved success was the continuing interest of some adult—a parent, a relative, a teacher, a social worker, a shop-owner, or a friend's parent. For almost everyone, sometime, somewhere, some adult had to be concerned about the young person in his growing up and had to help him with a word of encouragement, with some advice and with listening to him in hours of need.

Professionals have known the importance of the adult to children and adolescents, particularly as a support outside the family. Why then are adults bypassed, and why then is the peer group expected to do more than is possible? Why is there such reliance on the efficacy of the peer group without adult contribution?

There actually are communities that have provided "drop-in centers" or storefront facilities for groups of young drug-users without adult or professional supervision. The rationale presented for this is the insistence by the young drug-users that they will not come if there is supervision. However, experience has shown that too often, when they come to such a facility, they do so to turn on with drugs in the back room, supported by the drug-using peer group, undeterred and unfrustrated by any dissenting adult voice.

THE SEDUCTION OF THE EX-ADDICT

To some extent the glorification of youth, and the belief that only the young can speak to the young, accounts for the developing reliance upon the ex-addict, who is usually young, in treatment of drug-users. But it does not sufficiently explain this present-day phenomenon.

It is quite common, when drug use is known, that treatment responsibility is relegated to the ex-addict, the peer group consisting of all drug-users, or the confrontation "expert," usually, again, an ex-addict. There are even treatment agencies focused on the drug-using adolescent who assign a professional to work with parents, but insist upon assigning an ex-addict for their children.

This new cadre of helpers usually has obtained its expertise in counseling through its own addiction and social failure. Consider the implication of the fact that their potential helping abilities are dependent upon their willingness to remain in the drug culture via their employment! Their healing skills, their knowledge of the personality of the drug-user, and their own recovery or abstinence, are taken for granted without the evidence to support it. On the contrary, there is a disquieting amount of evidence to the contrary, including the frequent occurrence of recidivism among former drug-users, even those who have become counselors.

Why then is there such optimism about the therapeutic potential of untrained ex-addicts? There is little evidence of their efficacy. Too many drug programs are notorious for resisting accountability or verification, or even providing statistical information in any reasonable way. The continuation of this myth—of the efficacy of the use of the ex-addict—has spread to the school where he, the school dropout, has frequently been presented with much fanfare at school assemblies on the drug problem. The intent is to have the gory picture of the life of the drug-abuser exposed and thus to deter drug use by other youths. However, in effect, deviant, self-destructive be-havior is being rewarded. The value to adolescent stu-dents has not been examined and the implicit education-al message of this exhibitionism for young people has only recently begun to be questioned.

You also have been subjected to television's exploita-tion of young people who have been encouraged by adults to exhibit themselves and their dereliction with-out consideration of its meaning in their developmental struggles and tasks. The American Psychiatric Associa-tion and the National Association for Mental Health have condemned the use of ex-addicts in drug-education programs as communicating a hidden agenda of glam-our and success associated with addiction to the TV and school audiences. They have found that the observer could only think that if the ex-addict had never taken heroin, he would never have been on TV, or have been making all that money running treatment centers. But the ex-addict is not to be blamed for how he is being used and abused. Others have the responsibility to help him find more constructive opportunities.

Though there are many complaints about professional therapeutic intervention, and it is often inadequate, who can believe that impulsive, untutored intervention, that is subject to neither ethical nor professional controls, can be better?

THE ENCOUNTER GROUP

The encounter or confrontation group has come to be regarded as a panacea. In this therapy, there is a pur-ported acceleration of "insights," supposedly acquired through confrontation with others, as well as experimen-tation in touching, smelling, doing, with little back-up support for the participant who may become agitated afterwards.

Many drug facilities rely upon confrontation. The confrontation expert again may be a young former addict. These "experts" have become the proponents of instant salvation or the speed that can kill. Some segments of the professional community have been appropriately concerned about this and have warned of the dangers of confrontation and encounter groups, particularly in the hands of the untrained and the unskilled. Recent research suggests that emotional disturbances, serious and mild, both transitory and enduring, may be precipitated by thoughtless encounter-group experiences. Such experiences are not confined to the drug scene nor to administration by nonprofessionals.

Professional societies have been increasingly concerned about the growing use of the encounter group, even by professionals. One of the problems lies in the indiscriminate prescription and use of this method for experience, kicks, or therapy—too often without any screening of the participants. It is as if a high-powered drug would be administered without examination or knowledge of the previous medical history of the individual. Even such a beneficial drug as penicillin cannot be taken by everybody. Physicians have learned by now to verify previous experiences with this or similar drugs.

These principles are applicable to the therapeutic scene. The choice of treatment must be related to understanding the individual's needs, which may include knowledge of his past history and must include an assessment of his strengths and weaknesses, and knowledge of his current life. This applies to the encounter group.

The encounter group tends to encourage continuation of the adolescent drug-user's predilection for thoughtless and impulsive behavior. It stresses feeling and expression, and manipulates the experiences of the individual in the group to enable him to be "freer." However, the adolescent drug-user is already struggling with the means of using freedom for his own best interests. He needs instead to learn to discriminate between freedom and license. Encouragement has to be circumscribed by considerations of when, where, and how. In addition, there are some young people whose adjustment to reality is so precarious that free expression of emotion is the last thing any thoughtful clinician would recommend.

For example, a young boy, nineteen years of age, with a long history of emotional disturbance, went to an encounter session where dance therapy was being used. He was told to dance out the killing of his mother. The rationale was to get to his unconscious hostility. After the session, he became hysterical, and he had to be hospitalized because he thought he really had killed his mother. His problem was exactly in the area of distinguishing between fantasy and reality, wish and deed. He needed help in facing reality, instead of living in the make-believe world of his troubled mind. This was not therapy. Instead, action was substituted for thought and understanding.

Another situation had a happier ending. A seventeen-year-old boy, again with a long history of emotional disturbance and only occasional impulsive drug use, was accepted by a drug residence where the specialty was encounter treatment. In his first encounter session he was thrown into a panic when he listened to confirmed addicts and pushers talk about the murders, robberies, and rapes they had committed. He felt he was going crazy when he heard of actual events that were too close to his own fears. Fortunately, he sought help from a trained therapist, who removed him from the group following a conversation with the eighteen-year-old ex-addict "facilitator." The therapist asked the facilitator what he thought his client's problems were and his plans for helping him. Did he know what was wrong? The reply was that he was an ex-addict and knew everything.

Group treatment under trained auspices as a means of assisting people in trouble, particularly adolescents, is another matter. Group experiences are valuable to help the individual to relate to others and to learn how to give and receive assistance in understanding problems and anxieties.

It is understandable that many people who have been subjected to media popularization of encounter should be moved by the immediate appeal of this product with all it promises in the face of the enormity of the drug problem. It is less understandable that professionals should tout it so vigorously when its safety, efficacy, and durability, particularly for youngsters who are not addicted, have not been tested over time.

BEFORE ADDICTION

Most often it is the parent of the adolescent who believes that some kind of help is necessary. It is seldom that the young person asks for therapy. Sometimes his school becomes concerned because of the way he is acting or performing within the school. The larger society may become involved when there is some kind of delinquency, which today frequently includes involvement with drugs, however minimal. Anyone of these problems may and usually does precede addiction. However, no one of these problems has to lead to addiction.

Though any regular drug use should be considered a warning sign that there is trouble, drug usage is not, in and of itself, a psychological entity, or a diagnostic category. It is not enough to assess people as drug-users or abusers. That would be like the physician who sees a man walking with a severe limp and then diagnoses him as having a sore leg. It tells nothing but the obvious. The physician looks for the causes of the disorder, such as fracture, muscle tear, arthritis, and nerve damage.

When a young person is involved in drug use, it is important to know not only the extent of that drug use, but also the possible cause. Though he may have been "socialized" into experimenting, this does not explain his particular reasons for indulging in more than that. Most frequently, drug use is an attempt to mask uncomfortable feelings or to avoid dealing with other life-problems. It may be part of a behavior pattern that is either impulsive or compulsive; he may not be able to control himself in many ways, including but not restricted to drug use.

Adolescents need to be seen as total people. Diagnosing them as drug-users, and subjecting them to additional and intensified contact with other drug-users, makes little sense.

One of the problems for the adolescent who is referred to a group of drug-users, is that such a group frequently has an investment in keeping people on drugs. The influence of this kind of homogeneous group too often is for continuing in the drug culture, rather than leaving it. When the user who is not yet an addict is involved with addicts who often don't really want to kick the habit, further corruption is possible. You have only to reflect on what happens to young delinquents when they are forced into close contact with hardened criminals. Then they learn more about crime. Similarly, contact with hardcore addicts is contaminating.

Can you accept that eight-year-olds and twelve-year-olds, should be treated as drug addicts? There are children in these age groups who have been referred to drug facilities to live in day-to-day contact with seventeen-to-nineteen-year-old addicts and to be tutored by not much older ex-addict therapists. Isn't it common sense that an eight-year-old needs less encounter, and more good parenting? If the latter is not available in his own home, substitute plans for good nutrition, good sleep, and good caring must be made. No therapist is an equivalent for a good parent in those years when this is essential; certainly, confused young people such as ex-addicts offer little possibility of objectivity, generational distance, or good role-models.

None of this is to say that therapy of the proper kind cannot be helpful. On the contrary, it is possible for therapy to supplement other good caring for children. But it can never be substituted for the appropriate and healthy environment everybody needs. It can be an additional support. It can assist adolescents to use their good thinking potentials in the service of their own lives, and it can help them make considered decisions for their future lives. It can also assist their parents and guardians better to understand them as well as themselves.

Therapy of this nature will not deal exclusively with the subject of drug use. It will go further and deeper. However, neither will there be neglect of the implications of drug use for the adolescent who may be using drugs; the prominence of drugs in today's adolescent society cannot be forgotten. What will be remembered will be the uniqueness of every individual. What will be enhanced will be his potentials for better living.

Therapy, in this sense, will be growth-producing. Because drug use so frequently interferes with growing and living, many young drug-users appear to have stopped at a less-than-optimal point. With the support of an appropriately trained, and objective older person, such youngsters should begin to grow again, and therefore to continue the necessary work of adolescense: finding out who they are and determining how they should be.

5. For Example: An Interview with an Adolescent

Drug use by adolescents is frequently caused by efforts to hide a variety of uncomfortable feelings, to forget a specific problem that seems insoluble, or to overcome feelings of depression.

Many adolescents struggle deeply with the questions, "Who am I? What will I become?" If they cannot satisfy themselves with an answer, they sometimes suffer from feelings of alienation and even unrelatedness. These feelings can seem unbearable. Not infrequently today, they then turn to drug-using, thinking they will find the answers there.

For example, Ellen, a seventeen-year-old girl, was sent for help because she had been using LSD almost weekly for a year. She thought she found meaning and excitement in drug-induced hallucinations that she could not find in real life. Her problems were in relation to what was really going on around her.

Under LSD she felt more alive and aware. Her feelings about herself and others seemed richer and stronger than in real life. She was failing every subject in school and had a bizarre, freaked-out appearance.

Ellen was able to do very well in therapy because she really wanted to know herself and her reality. Treatment was better than drugs, which only told her about fantasies. As she became interested in exploring her inner feelings, she became more self-aware. She then returned to complete her formal education so that she would not remain ignorant and could make wiser choices about her future. In this example, her real problem was an acute feeling of alienation. This painful feeling was temporarily relieved by taking LSD. The drug use, however, directly interfered with her natural growth and development.

Some adolescents use drugs to get even with their parents if they are angry with them, knowing this makes many parents feel worried and disgraces them.

For example, Roberta was seen by a social worker after she had become known to the court because of a gang fight. She readily confided great resentment toward her mother and subsequently related that she was both taking and selling various drugs in her community. Her anger was so great that she had even become involved in serious criminal behavior. Here drugs were used to disgrace her parents through antisocial behavior, again as a way of temporarily resolving unpleasant feelings.

In this instance, placement in a carefully chosen school away from home where she could continue treatment was arranged because it was too dangerous for her to work on her problems at home when she could not control her anger toward her parents. This was decided upon in consultation with her parents. All agreed that it would be safer for her to be removed from contact with her old friends as well, because they were a bad influence which she was not strong enough or sufficiently mature to withstand.

At school, away from home, she continued her formal education, and in addition spent much time studying herself and her angry feelings. The goal was for her to learn how she could help herself rather than hurting herself.

Her parents also spent the time studying themselves in therapy. They tried to understand where they might have gone wrong, how they could help Roberta and in the process help themselves.

Getting a young adolescent involved in a treatment situation usually has difficulties. Because it usually is some authority, you, or a teacher or some other older adult who suggests therapy to him, he often will at first see this as a criticism or putdown. He may then respond by turning it into a rebellious power struggle.

However, if he can see that from the beginning this is something about which in the long run he will have to make the final judgment, he may be willing to try. Sometimes you may be able to convince him that it is really more intelligent to find out for himself.

If you can convince him in one way or another to give it a try, and then if he takes the first step to find out, he usually is in for a pleasant surprise. In addition, chances are he is a good candidate. Many young people are introspective, philosophical, sensitive, and verbal. All of these are assets for using psychological help.

Frequently people need a period of exploration in the beginning of therapy when they are less certain about what they want to achieve. Until they know, they seldom wish to make any longterm commitment. Adolescents, particularly, are at a time of life when they do not wish to be tied down to anything on a regular basis over a long period of time. Thinking ahead into the future is difficult for young people. Therefore they should not be expected to commit themselves to a longterm arrangement.

The adolescent has to know that when he wishes to stop therapy, even if there is a difference of opinion, he will have the right to have his opinion considered, and in the long run his decision honored. In addition, young people frequently may need breathers during which time they put into practice some of the things they have been learning. Among the things they will learn is the fact that they can leave; therefore they can come back when it is helpful for themselves. Thus stops and starts are not unusual in therapeutic practice with adolescents. In any event, the most important thing is for him to eventually make the process his own and to want to come for himself and not because he is being pressured by someone else.

Therapy will be a new situation, and like other new and unknown experiences it may seem frightening. Your child needs to know what to expect of the experience even before he starts, so that it may be less awesome. He needs to know that it is basically a verbal situation. It consists of talk—no needles, gadgets, gimmicks, or machines. The process involves facing yourself; it is based on the ancient notion "know thyself." Sometimes this is frightening because of a fear of finding out some unpleasant facts about oneself; just as frequently, there are hidden strengths to be discovered.

The adolescent may also wonder about his privacy and whether his confidences will be revealed to his parents or other authorities. The professional practice in regard to confidentiality is not to reveal any information without signed consent of the person involved. Some states which license professionals who do therapy grant them the same legal rights of privileged information as are granted to clergymen, lawyers, and physicians.

Usually parents are not contacted without the knowledge and consent of the young person involved. Some do not mind if their parents see the same person as they are, some prefer they be seen by someone else, and some may want to be present when their parents are seen. In any case, their feelings will be respected.

It is helpful for an adolescent to be seen by someone who is older than he is by many years. It can be a valuable experience for him to have a relationship with a nonfamilial adult who will make a serious effort to understand him and his lifestyle. Explaining his rationale and making himself understood will also be helpful for him. He will usually like having the individual attention of someone who will work with him for his welfare in a friendly and interested manner. However, most therapists will refrain from being more than that and will tend not to be too revealing of themselves or their own lives. This is not because they try to be cold or aloof, but because experience has taught that it is more helpful for there to be some distance, which enables objectivity. *

If a therapist is totally mod or with it or overfriendly, he might as well be a friend. Friends are helpful, and particularly important for young people. However, they cannot provide therapy because they are probably having the same struggles and problems. It is better then to see someone who, in addition to not being involved in similar difficulties, has been professionally educated to assist in solving those problems.

Perhaps it might be helpful in trying to explain how therapy works to provide a synopsis of a first meeting with a seventeen-year-old girl. As is customary in instances where actual case material is discussed, all identifying information has been disguised.

THE EXAMPLE

Doris came to see a social worker on the advice of her mother's psychiatrist. Her mother had told her own therapist that following a weekend visit by Doris with a friend, she had unpacked Doris's suitcase and found a birth control device in it. Doris denied it was hers, but her mother did not believe her story and asked her psychiatrist to see Doris. It was suggested that Doris should be asked if she wanted this or if she would prefer to see someone else. Doris said that she preferred to speak with someone other than her mother's psychiatrist. The following is an account of her first meeting with Mrs. X.

MRS. X: Hello, I'm Mrs. X.

DORIS: Hello.

(They enter the office and are seated opposite each other

in armchairs. A therapy room looks much like a study and is usually furnished with easy chairs, a couch, books, and a telephone.)

MRS. X: I understand that you were referred by Dr. Y, who is working with your mother. Dr. Y told me that you might be calling me for an appointment, and that your mother was concerned about you. That's all I know, so perhaps you can tell me more about why you are here.

DORIS: Well, it's really all my mother. She worries, but it is all her own fault. You see, I was away a couple of weeks ago. I stayed with my friend Emily at her home, for a weekend visit. After I got back, my mother unpacked my bag. I didn't tell her to, it was just lying around in my room. Anyway, she found a diaphragm there and she got very upset. She really hassled me, wanting to know if I was having sex, lecturing me that I'm too young, that's all.

MRS. X: What did you tell your mother?

DORIS: Oh, that it wasn't mine, that Emily had gotten it and was afraid her mother would find it and I agreed to take it home with me.

MRS. X: And your mother didn't believe you?

DORIS: No, not really.

MRS. X: Should she have?

DORIS: Well, I suppose not. But I didn't want to tell her. She just would have been more upset. It's not her business if I have sex, and she shouldn't have gone into my bag. But she was upset anyway.

MRS. X: So I guess the diaphragm was yours. Would you care to tell me about it?

DORIS: (Pause). O.K. You see, it was the other way around. A few months ago I met a boy at a party at Emily's house. I really liked him; we liked

each other. He was going into the army in a little while. We wanted to sleep with each other.
Well, anyway, I wanted to sleep with him, have
an affair. I knew he would be going away soon.
So I planned it. I went to a doctor where Emily
lives to get the diaphragm. I used to meet him
when I would visit Emily. Now, anyway, he's
gone. Maybe I'll see him, I don't know.

MRS. X: Then, of course, since you got a diaphragm
for this affair, you were not a virgin.

DORIS: No, not since last year. But just once, because I
didn't want to be a virgin.

MRS. X: Why not? What bothers you about being a virgin?

DORIS: What bothers me? I just didn't want to be one.

MRS. X: Were you in love?

DORIS: No, we liked each other, but we knew this was
just for a while.

MRS. X: So you're saying your sexual activity doesn't
bother you, but it bothers your mother that you
might be having sex.

DORIS: That's right. She really lectures me, all the time.
She tells me about diseases, dangers, constantly
talking at me about not having sex, not being
promiscuous. I don't want to talk about it any-
more.

MRS. X: O.K. What else does she lecture you about?

DORIS: School. School is another big thing.

MRS. X: In what way?

DORIS: Well, sometimes, I like school, I mean I like a
few teachers and a few courses. But mostly I
don't.

MRS. X: What don't you like?

DORIS: Most of the teachers, the way they treat the stu-
dents. Some of them are incompetent, so they
don't give the kids a chance. I mean, they are

afraid if the kids want to do something new or different. Some of the books we read in English, for instance, are not relevant. But if the teachers are poor, they make you stick to the same subjects and give the same interpretations to the same material. They are afraid of anything new.

MRS. X: What should they do to be more effective teachers?

DORIS: I think that they should listen more to the kids, not force their opinions so much, maybe even let the kids run a class sometimes. I guess I'll go to college. I mean it's just expected by my parents. My dad's a lawyer, he just takes it for granted. But my mother is always telling me about getting into a good college, doing very good so that I can make a better school, how important that is. I am in two honors classes but I don't really like them; they are an awful lot of work. We really need to put in a lot of time in the library, there is a lot of reading. I'm in English and history honors. And I am thinking of dropping the history because it is just too much. The amount of work expected I mean. In a way it's the same with school. Last week we had to take a test about our vocational choices. Many of the kids were really scared and upset. They didn't tell us what it was for, and some of the kids thought it would affect their future or getting into college. I didn't care. When it came to first choice for vocation I wrote down "steeplejack."

MRS. X: Well, it's wrong to push kids so hard. You shouldn't have to make decisions you're not ready for.

DORIS: A lot of kids were really shook up about that.

MRS. X: I can see why.But you know you have been telling me that you feel pressured not only just in school but mainly by your mother. Is that right?

DORIS: Yes

MRS. X: Then how would you say you and your mother get along?

DORIS: So-so. If I don't tell her things or if I can handle her, not listen to her, it's O.K. But she finds out about things, or sometimes she really gets to me and it gets bad.

MRS. X: Like now. Are you here because she has pressured you?

DORIS: She did, but I was willing to come here.

MRS. X: Then I wonder if you would want to continue to come for a while? I think that you have a problem with your mother, that you and she don't get along as well as you should. If you would like to try seeing me for a few months, perhaps we can explore what happens between you two and how you deal with each other. I think you're pretty angry with her because things are always such a strain for you. Maybe there is a better way to get along if you understood yourself better, and her too. What do you think?

DORIS: All right, but I'll come only until school ends in three months.

MRS. X: That's a good amount of time. At the end we'll decide together if you want to stop or go further. Let's set up a weekly appointment.

As you read this, you could see what went on. A young girl who feels pushed by her mother and other adults, also feels very angry with them. At the same time, she pushed herself into sexual activity, yet lets her mother find evidence of her sex life, knowing very well it will offend her mother's moral code. You have probably wondered how a mother of a seventeen-year-old unpacked her suitcase. This mother did, and always had, and Doris knew it. Thus, one might question, if she were old enough to have sex, shouldn't she have been old enough to keep it private?

What Mrs. X felt was not a judgment about whether or not Doris should have sex, but a question about how Doris was using sex. It seemed to her that something might be wrong, since Doris seemed so calculating and unemotional about sex and did not seem to have any feelings for the boys involved. Rather, she appeared to be using sex in a provocative way. Yet when Doris did not want to talk about it any more, Mrs. X respected her wish, knowing with certainty that as she trusted more, the problem would come up again. She also wanted to concentrate now on the unhappy relationship between Doris and her mother because this seemed to be the basic problem. When she did, Doris agreed with her and was willing to begin on this basis. The fact that Doris's mother was also in therapy was a big asset in this case, for she too needed help to understand her contribution to the difficulties in their relationship.

In the ensuing months, Doris talked about all the pressures she was experiencing for high performance from her mother at home and from teachers at school. Gradually she spoke of her feelings of inadequacy; she wasn't smart enough to be accepted by and to be comfortable at the "good" colleges they wanted for her; she was afraid of going anyway. She felt pressured by peers to experiment with drugs. She had used marijuana, she had tried speed, and some of her friends wanted her to try LSD. She felt she would be square to refuse even though she was afraid to try. She also did not feel as pretty as other girls and felt very unsure of herself with boys.

Doris stayed in treatment more than three months— long enough to better understand herself and to be able to communicate her feelings.

This is just one example of what is called psychotherapy. But people are helped by varying kinds of individual and group experiences. Psychotherapy is not for everyone. There will always be people in need of therapeutic help, and it is unrealistic to suppose that there will ever be enough professional manpower to meet this need.

However, no adolescent should be allowed to chemically lobotomize himself and to feel nothing. Rather, he should be assisted to learn to struggle with the great internal and external issues of life.

6. Therapy and the Parents of Adolescents

It is not easy to decide to choose therapy as a means of helping your child.

The idea of seeking help from an outsider is itself difficult and anxiety-producing. For some of you it may seem to threaten your own independence and adequacy, even though you may be intellectually aware that all people need help from others.

When your children were younger it was easy for you to share your concerns and to talk with neighbors, friends, and relatives about the solutions they had found to problems with children. It was simpler to express worry then, or fear, or anger, when Johnny or Mary wouldn't try new foods, had trouble sleeping, or was slow or stubborn about learning to use the bathroom rather than diapers. You did not feel as ashamed then as you may feel now.

For one thing, when the children still needed to be supervised all the time, you had more opportunity to talk with other parents. Then you simply spent more time together. This encouraged more exchange about what you had in common at the moment, which was your children. You all talked about problems with your Johnnys and Marys, because you all wanted to know better how to bring them up. In addition, you generally believed that whatever the problems, they were transitory and would be outgrown; there was quite a long time ahead before they would be grownup.

Some among you were very concerned about why your very young child was not doing some of the things other children had already mastered. You might have felt that he was having some behavior difficulty, but more often than not you found some support from another parent. It was relatively easy then to talk with a friend who offered assurance that it would work out and who told you about some other child who had gone through pretty much the same thing and had outgrown it. In most instances, you were helped to feel that you need not be afraid or guilty because Johnny or Mary was not very different from so many other children. Growing up normally had some problems, but you realized these were phases most children experienced. After all, you yourself had probably gone through many of the same things, and you were all right. And at that time your children were still very young. It was very clear that your children needed you and your closeness to them because they needed to be taken care of. This gave you more of a sense of control, that you were present to help guide and shape what was going on.

Asking for help and getting it then, when the children were smaller, did not have the same urgency and opprobrium as it may seem to have now. Then the problems were more often within the home and in relation to you. Now, they are not only within the home, but outside as well, so that these problems have become noticeable to others and even dangerous for your child.

The type of therapy that you as well as anybody else can use is one that respects you and your contributions, past and present. It operates under the assumption that if young people are to be helped, particularly those whose problems are complicated by drug use, you, as the parent, need to participate in the helping process. Furthermore, while your children live at home, they still depend upon you, and you are needed to help others understand them.

Another assumption is that without your help the chances for a successful outcome are significantly reduced. This kind of therapy will help you decide the best way to help your child.

There are other kinds of therapy that will make you feel even more of a failure. If you happen upon this, you will feel that you and you alone are to blame for your child's difficulties. Sometimes you may receive directives for your behavior which may seem not to fit your particular situation and which you may find impossible to implement. This kind of therapy will immobilize you, and add to your sense of failure. You may come away from such an experience feeling more to blame and more hopeless.

If you have ever sought help from experts before and if this has happened to you, you should consider whether you have seen the right person or have sought the right kind of help. After all, when anyone makes a decision to seek some kind of therapeutic intervention, he is already sufficiently unhappy. He doesn't need more unhappiness. Of course, if this has happened to you many times, you have probably reached the stage of wondering whether there is anything you do to precipitate this result. It is unfortunate, but sometimes this may happen.

FEELING A FAILURE

It is not uncommon to have had smooth sailing when the kids were little and to find that things are just too much when your children reach adolescence.

Your children who seemed to be making it all right in the lower grades may suddenly seem to be having trouble in school, in passing courses or by playing hookey. Many of you may not even know about it until virtually the end of the term. When you do go to school to talk about their poor school performance, don't you find that inevitably the conversation gets around to what is going on at home? No matter what you may think of the teacher, no matter what the tenor of the discussion, you somehow end up feeling as if it is your fault and you have failed? You may have tried to repress your reactions to what is going on in the school. In a few instances, the school may have personnel who are interested and qualified to begin to sort out with you how you and the school together may search for ways to help your child out of his dilemma. Unfortunately, this opportunity is available to only a very few within the school.

Without this support, it is very hard to deal constructively with your own confused and chaotic feelings—the same feelings reflected, it may seem to you, in the chaos you may have experienced in the school because of the open corridors and laissez-faire atmosphere.

On top of Johnny's not doing well, all this freedom cannot but exacerbate your worry about your child's budding sexuality and your knowledge that sexual mores are changing rapidly; the attitudes and feelings of "good" kids themselves about sexual experimentation are very different from yours.

So where is it for you? Your youngster is doing poorly in school and you have been led to believe you are largely responsible. You are worried enough about your adolescent's becoming a sexual being and either becoming pregnant or irresponsibly siring a child. In addition, the threat of drugs is all around.

At home your child is sullen, sad, and solitary. You worry about that, too, because you have a notion that at this time in his life, friends are very important. While Johnny or Mary has been behaving somewhat more strangely lately and looking even more apart at the seams, are you afraid to say anything more because it doesn't seem to make a difference to your child?

You have read that one explanation for destructive adolescent behavior is that parents are too controlling, or is it not sufficiently disciplining? More important you are a little shook by the terribly angry feelings that are beginning to stir inside you. The truth of it is that you do feel you have failed. Even worse, you do not know how to move to get out of the box in which you find yourself. What you have tried to read only adds to your confusion. It seems that no matter to whom you talk, you end up feeling you are the guilty one.

TROUBLE AT HOME

Even your spouse may begin to feel like an enemy because his or her discomfort is so great. Suddenly you are saying angry things to each other which may have been unspoken for a long time. Somehow Johnny's or Mary's difficulties seem to blow the lid from a keg of dynamite, and you are shocked by the intensity of your pain and anger. All this comes at a time when you may be struggling with the meaning to you of getting older, both physically and psychologically. For mother it may mean that her primary importance in the family, raising children, is coming to an end, and there isn't even the promised reward of seeing that she did well. If you have not given some thought and planning to what will be, there is as yet little on the horizon which promises to fill an anticipated vacuum. For father, there may be real concern about how adequately his prior labors and projected ones will provide in the still far-off prospect of retirement. Business has been rough, unemployment rates are rising, inflation seems uncontrollable, the problems of the country seem overwhelming, and there is still Bill to get through school. What is going on in the world does not begin to compare with your anguished feelings about the problems at home.

Coming home or, as the case may be, being at home may begin to take on the overtones of dread—not because there are problems, because most of you have continually dealt with problems which, in one way or another, seemed to have worked out, and you have had a sense of your own ability to cope, but rather, because you begin to get the feeling of being trapped. No matter what has been tried, it does not seem to work. One does not mind the struggle so much if it is balanced with some pleasure and, most important, with the expectation that within the not-too-distant future, things will be better. But now you may be faced with the feeling that you really would rather be anyplace but home. The atmosphere there may be filled with open conflict—you and your spouse together against Johnny or Mary; you and your spouse against each other, seemingly because of Johnny or Mary. Or the atmosphere may be one of silence about important problems. Knowingly or unknowingly, you may have chosen to avoid saying the "terrible" things you are startled to realize you are capable of thinking. The way you experience distress and manage it more often than not reflects your style of communication with both yourself and others, which has developed over time. Perhaps the most stressful element is the awareness of feelings of rage, even hatred, of which you are capable toward these family members whom you also love, want, and need.

So you are at an impasse. Your child isn't making it, you are feeling helpless to help him, and everybody is miserable.

THE BEGINNING OF THERAPY

You may decide to look for some outside professional counseling. To begin with, the most obvious thing to do is to obtain a recommendation about where to go from a person you respect and who you believe knows something about the subject. He might suggest a social agency, a psychotherapy institute, or a private practitioner who may be a psychiatrist, a psychologist, or a social worker.

In any case, it is a good idea to begin with a consultation to decide upon the best course for you and your family. This should certainly involve both mother and father. It also is very helpful if you can convince your youngster to come along, so that he is in at the beginning and can help to make the decisions that will need his cooperation. This is not always possible, particularly when you are having trouble with him anyway. Sometimes you can learn from the consultation how and when to involve him, and even get some help in doing so.

There are even times when, as the result of the consultation, you may conclude that you really do not have a problem with your child. After talking about the difficulty, you may discover that you have been worrying needlessly. You may also decide that it is better to continue and to do something to help him.

If the decision you make is to see someone on a one-to-one basis, what can you expect?

First, he will be aware that the decision to come to an outsider is extremely difficult and that you may be unsure of what to expect. In addition, he will understand that you may be feeling two ways about having made the decision: wanting to find out what it's about and wishing you had never come.

In the beginning it is appropriate to ask about his qualifications, his experience, and whether he thinks he can be of help. Because many of you may seek help later rather than sooner, there is the great temptation to buy him too easily on faith and to expect magic; this may be because of the degree of your stress and the sense of relief that can come with finally finding a place to relieve overburdened feelings. While he may be skilled in helping, he has no magic to offer. Rather, he can put at your disposal his knowledge about how people try to deal with problems. He will try to help you understand and evaluate how your family goes about working out its difficulties.

Therapists place great value on maximizing possibilities for young people's growth. They generally believe that this takes place best in an atmosphere which values connectedness and responsibility. For this it will be necessary to understand as clearly as possible what is going on in the family situation as this affects you and your youngsters, particularly in areas where there are problems. It will be recognized that because perception is subjective, both your point of view and that of your child will need to be understood. Experience suggests that younger adolescents really welcome their parents' participation and usually perceive this as evidence of their caring, despite any initial comments to the contrary. They are not ready, nor do they really want, to be completely separated from their families.

Depending on the circumstances, you may be seen with your youngster or separately. Decisions about how to plan for future contacts will depend on a series of considerations, among which are the youngster's age and his readiness to talk to the same person to whom his parents are speaking. Younger adolescents usually want their parents involved. For the older adolescent for whom separation may be central to the conflict in a way appropriate to his age, resisting parental involvement may be both necessary and healthy. As a result, the decision may be reached that you will meet with someone different from the person seeing your child.

Decisions will also have to be made about whether group or individual contacts are desirable, and for whom. In addition, how parents are to be involved, whether you will be seen together with your spouse or separately, and who will see whom—all these things need to be discussed. These decisions depend upon a variety of considerations: the nature of the problems, the feelings of the people involved, and the reality of what facilities are available to accommodate these choices.

Whatever the decision, it should be clear from the beginning that the content of these meetings is confidential. If more than one therapist becomes involved, the process of helping moves better when they communicate with each other. This enables you to have some general notions from them about how your children are doing, as well as to learn generally about that against which your youngsters are reacting. This communication between therapists is particularly important when the inability to communicate is a major problem in the relationship. Under no circumstances should you be totally excluded. Ways must be found to help your child, who may be seen separately, to accept the necessity for some appropriate communication by his therapist to you, either via the person you are seeing, in a telephone call, or in a family conference. If your experience is different, and if you feel excluded, you should feel free to discuss this, so that a mutual understanding may be reached by everyone involved.

This is a particularly important point. Sometimes therapists identify with the perceptions expressed by angry children of their parents. Then they may believe you are an ogre. If they are experienced in working with young people and if they understand, as they should, the difficulties of parent-child relationships during adolescence, this will not happen. However, sometimes, it does happen, and it may happen to you. There is no reason why you should ever allow yourself to be forcibly excluded from your child's life by outsiders, particularly when they still expect you to pay their bills. If this ever happens to you, you are probably involved in a kind of debilitating therapy. There is no reason for you to take such distasteful and harmful medicine.

In the beginning, you probably will be asked to talk about what is going on and also be asked questions to direct your thinking. This frequently is of help. Through this telling you usually can see more clearly what is happening and how it has developed. As time goes on, you may be asked how it was when you grew up, so that both your own experience and expectations will be better understood. This may have some bearing on what is going on in the present.

Sometimes, as a result of parents' having grown up in quite different circumstances from their children, there are differences in attitudes, feelings, and perceptions which need to be understood and reconciled if possible. You may be asked particularly about your own adolescence and what you recall of it. The objective would be to have you remember as much as you can. Sometimes this will help you understand and be more sympathetic about that which is troubling your child, even though he is not coping adequately.

You may be asked about other areas of your life, such as work, marriage, other children, and other important people to better understand what stresses may be affecting the family. You also will be encouraged to speak freely about any problems with which you are struggling at the particular moment that you feel you need to talk about. Through this process some of your frustration and anger may be reduced. You will be able then to decide where it is best to focus your efforts and what areas of the problem need examination at the moment.

At no time should you be given the impression that you are being judged. Most people in the helping professions are usually impressed by the strengths shown by so many parents, considering the extent of their personal and family problems. Whatever has gone on before, however difficult the relationships within your family, it should be accepted that you want to see your children grow and create lives for themselves which are satisfying to them and to you as their parents.

However, as parents you may not agree with all of your children's choices. Decisions about which of them you will strongly oppose and which you will support will have to be made. You will probably find satisfaction in choosing to do some things differently because of your increased understanding, but no one will expect you to be a different person from that which you are. Usually you will experience considerably more clarity about who you are and what you want to do for yourself as well as for your children. This should make for a more comfortable managing of your life.

Of course it will not be easy to come to terms with your inconsistencies if they exist. When you have someone to talk to who will care about what happens to you, however, it becomes increasingly possible to look reality squarely in the face. It also becomes easier to evaluate how things can be improved in your family. Most important, you will have the added ingredient of hope that things can be better.

You will be asked about specifics of family living. When there are patterns of family interaction and responses which may not be the most realistic, they will be pointed out. You will be asked to test out whether these observations are accurate. This usually helps you to become more attuned to what is going on. Communication will probably turn out to be a major focus of the work you will do. It is very common for families in difficulty to have a tendency to give each other mixed messages, both verbally and nonverbally. Though you may be able to do very well in a variety of enterprises, sometimes when it comes to intimate interactions in the family your conscious wishes to see your children do better may have some other components of conflictual feelings, and these will be communicated. This becomes particularly apparent in family sessions which can help to pinpoint the kinds of mixed messages that are being sent and received.

Perhaps some examples will help to point up how difficult it is at times to come to grips with what is felt as contrasted to what is said and done. This is particularly true when there is a great deal of stress and feelings are intense.

Mr. and Mrs. S knew that fifteen-year-old Denny had been popping pills. They had spent considerable time with his therapist discussing the appropriate amounts needed to meet Denny's everyday expenses but not to allow extra money for drugs. Subsequently, Mr. and Mrs. S announced that they had decided to increase Denny's allowance as his birthday present. It should be no surprise that the basis of the decision-making and the needs that were being met became the subject of considerable exploration. In this instance, it was not sufficient merely to decide not to increase Denny's allowance. It was apparent that there were repeated instances when behavior was contradictory to the parents' stated intentions. This served to confuse Denny in his efforts to figure out what really were his parents' expectations.

Then there is the situation of Mr. & Mrs. J who were advised by local suburban school authorities that Jack, age fifteen, had been buying marijuana in New York City for sale to his friends. The parents sought help, and the subject of providing adequate supervision because they were both working became a focus of early discussion. This was an expressed concern and the topic of considerable planning. Four weeks later, Mr. & Mrs. J let the therapist know that they had spent a long weekend in Washington, leaving Jack at home without adult supervision. In this instance, the contradiction between their expressed concern that their son be supervised and their decision to leave him at home alone for a weekend, needed to be faced and understood.

Mr. and Mrs. L brought their seventeen-year-old daughter for therapy after she informed them she had been using heroin irregularly for over a year and that she wanted help in stopping. Her parents had agreed to weekly sessions for their daughter. As a result, they recognized some improvement in her behavior. Suddenly the mother began to cancel her daughter's appointments with the excuse of having to do essential shopping which took "so much time and money." The meaning of Mrs. L's choices for her daughter and her ambivalence about having her daughter come for help had to be clarified. Her conscious wishes to provide the necessary protection to Joyce to maintain her beginning improvement needed to be supported and encouraged. This also involved greater understanding on the part of both parents of the depression and despair their daughter had been experiencing prior to her experimentation with heroin.

Mr. and Mrs. K, both highly successful professionals, prided themselves on their independent thinking and were well known for their critical judgment of existing institutions. They came for help when Robert, age sixteen and a former honors student, was failing math and doing below average work in his other subjects. They reported that they had agreed with Robert's criticism of the way in which subjects were taught and perceived this as evidence of his good critical judgment. They had known of their son's occasional absences and had given unspoken approval to his lack of regular attendance on the basis that their very bright child should not have to be bored. They avoided questioning what really was going on in school and what Robert was doing when out of classes. Only when they had to face knowing that he was a chronic truant and was using this time to relieve boredom by drug experimentation, did they begin to act constructively on their concern. They learned that their contempt and criticism had made Robert contemptuous of his teachers and authority. They recognized that as bright as he was, he was only sixteen and there really was much for him to learn. They decided that they needed to help him explore with the school ways to enrich his learning experience.

Whenever your adolescent is in trouble today, regardless of the difficulty, it is very important that you be aware that drugs might be compounding the difficulty. As a result, it would be wise if you actively inquired of him whether he is experimenting with or using drugs. It would be helpful if you take a stand firmly against such use and consistently follow through with decisions and behavior that affirm this position. This is necessary if you wish to work to eliminate drug usage. There is a lot of confusion based in part on the irrationality of the marijuana laws and the proliferation of literature pro and con. This is one of your dilemmas. But for your thirteen, fourteen, and fifteen-year-old you need not have any conflict. If their functioning is sufficiently impaired that you have decided to come for help, even marijuana may be a means of their avoiding their necessary facing up to the reality that they are not making it. This is an essential step if you are to begin to work on improvement of their behavior.

This step may be the first of many about which you will have conflict and ambivalence. You should have the opportunity to share these two-way feelings. Probably you will have to understand better why, around some issues, you can't say No even though all your good reasoning dictates the need to set limits. In contrast, questions and issues will arise that trigger an automatic No and about which you will agree one might legitimately argue.

Essentially, your work in therapy should affirm your rights as parents who are concerned about your children. It should help you better to understand the nature of the interaction within your family and to identify those attitudes and behavior patterns that are productive and those that seem to trigger a whole sequence of events which are counterproductive to all participants.

THERAPY IS A PROCESS

One of the most difficult challenges to you will be to accept the notion that this is a process and that results that are tangible may take time. Thus, for example, even though you take a stand with your child against drug experimentation and usage, there is no guarantee that he will stop immediately. In some instances it does happen, because this is all these young people need. In others, changes will have to be accompanied by improved attitudes within your youngster about himself. However, you can help to move them along. Further, it will be one among a number of examples through which he will become clearer about your readiness to really struggle with where it's at for you in relation to him, as well as for yourself.

In the process of trying to help your adolescent, a number of your own problems are bound to come up. Inevitably you will want to talk about a number of important relationships, one of the most important being your marriage. Most of you have read about the variety of ways couples struggle to maintain a balance in marriage and how children are too often caught up in this struggle. This may or may not be your problem, but frequently small shifts in feeling and behavior between spouses are very effective in altering family balance significantly enough to help your child.

If problems in the marriage should surface, it is basically your decision as to whether and how this becomes a part of your therapy. If serious discontent has been kept under wraps, it is logical that in a climate that places value on being strong enough to face problems, such discontent may well become apparent. It is logical, too, that there may be conflictual feelings around what you will discuss though there is the expectation that you will try to be as open as possible.

Inevitably, there will be times when you will question whether you wish to continue. This may be because you feel everything is better; if this is really so, everyone will probably agree with your wish. Sometimes you may feel it is too expensive, too time-consuming, and you may even wonder if it is worth all the trouble. And there will be times when nothing will seem to be happening.

Whatever you decide, in the long run it is your decision and your choice. However, one of the early conditions that is usually made when you begin will be that if you ever wish to stop, you will discuss your feelings before you put your decision into effect.

In the long run your decision to become involved in a form of therapy is really a decision to study your way of life, and since you are a parent, also the lives of your children. This is a very personal experience.

It should pay off in terms of better living for you and yours.

Part III
Therapy Is Not Enough

7. The Ecology of Human Beings

Children are natural resources.

Children are as important to the continuation and re-vitalization of the social environment as the woods and the lakes are to the physical environment. Pollution threatens the physical environment, the trees and the waters. Pollution also threatens the social environment and the children.

When your children were babies you worked hard to protect them. You kept them from all things that you thought were bad for them and tried to surround them with those things that were wholesome and good. You knew that the world was all new to them, and in their newness, your children did not know what they were seeing.

At the beginning, for your children, the world was fuzzy. You wanted to help them learn to know what was in the small world around them. You wanted to help them to understand what they were seeing. You did your best to help them to learn to cope with their world, small as it was.

Many of you stimulated your children to use their developing facilities. Do you remember how you introduced them to lights and darks, and colors and different shapes; how you helped them to take their first steps, and encouraged and aided the first words?

The same things apply to your child now that he is older and an adolescent. He still needs help in understanding and coming to grips with his world; he, too, has many new things to learn. It is at this time that he is changing so fast that he has to learn about himself; he also has to learn about a world that extends far from his home, one much bigger than he ever knew before.

Everyone has always known about these new challenges; all adolescents have had it. But the world adolescents, including yourself, once had to cope with was never so big. Today's adolescent really has to think about the four corners of the world because they are important to his daily living, and he has to learn to deal with this totality.

All the ways you protected your adolescent and all the things you tried to teach him when he was a baby, and then a child, were to prepare him to cope with this time of life and what you thought would come with it. You probably thought that at a certain time he would become an adult and he would have certain responsibilities and privileges. The world for which you were preparing him was simpler and clearer than the one he is in today. In many ways you are not now so experienced and so prepared to help.

Yet, you originally knew that you would have to help him through the period of adolescence, too, until he became an adult. You were fully aware that despite all the care, he could not have acquired the experience to cope with the many new dimensions he would be perceiving. You hoped he would see the world clearly, so he could learn to cope with it effectively. You have always thought he would need caring in adolescence, different from, yet similar to, his younger years.

Today your adolescent's problem in learning and your problem in caring are more difficult than you had envisaged. The world is less clear than ever before and it whizzes by so fast that it is hard to take hold of it. So much is happening, and so quickly. All dimensions of life are affected by constant change. As a result, everyone is constantly bombarded by new realities and new sensations that call for a constant reordering of thought and management.

For example, think of the significance of atomic energy. Though your adolescent has grown up in a world where the atomic bomb has always existed, this was not true for you. No young generation, ever before, has had to consider the possibility of its nonexistence.

On the other hand, the peaceful potentials of atomic energy, the implications for technology and productivity, also exist. The existence of these two disparate aspects of one factor of modern life are almost mind-blowing in the demands they make for priority planning. This presents problems to be solved and coped with in his adulthood, which is around the corner.

The issues are not so clear; the solutions perplexing.

Your child needs a clear view of the world. For that, he needs a clear mind.

And you have less control over what your adolescent child sees and how he sees it than any parent of an adolescent ever before.

TV

Your child's adolescence is very different from the adolescence of earlier generations. He has grown up with TV; his is the generation of the tube, the picture, and the vision. Yes, your generation had the radio and the movies, and they were influential in introducing you to things you would not have known of within the circle of your immediate home.

But the picture in the home has brought the world into the living room and into the life of your child. He is bombarded by quickly changing styles of life, morals, and values. He sees the glorification of many notorious individuals in television interviews; he has seen murder and assassination live.

Your adolescent watches television and sees the message of what he needs and what he should want. When he was a child he was seduced by toys and cereals, which he tried to seduce you to get for him. What he wants now is not that easy for you to give and for him to get.

The television commercials not only show him what he should buy to wear, and how to wear it. They also show him how not to care if it is too much for him to try. They show him how to slow down, pep up, ease off, cop out. There are drug-pushers on TV who are tempting your child into a stupor.

Tuning in can lead to turning off by turning on.

THE TEMPTATION

The temptation is to retreat from the stimuli that come too fast to allow for integration—for everybody, but particularly for the inexperienced. There are too many alternatives to be evaluated—for everybody, particularly for the inexperienced. There are too many important decisions that have to be made—particularly by the inexperienced.

The temptation is to retreat into a stupor. The addiction-vulnerability of the upcoming generation has roots in the desire to retreat into a cloud so as not to see and to feel and see only what it wishes. Not to see and not to feel makes it easy not to do.

Everybody—you too—has been tempted not to see. For a long time, the old adage—Out of sight, out of mind—has been in operation.

You had become used to daily reporting of robbery, assaults, and corruption in the slums of large cities. You had been able to read these reports with equanimity, as long as the peace of your own homes and neighborhoods remained undisturbed. Out of sight, who minded?

Even if you cared and knew that society needed to care for problems of others who were less fortunate, crime, drug abuse, and addiction were not real for you. But now the slums are no longer containing their problems. The distance between suburb and city has been shortened by the growth of each and by the speed of travel. There is no possible separation; there is no hiding place.

Every day the young drug-user is becoming younger and younger, and not only in the slums. The drug-dealing of the ghetto has moved into even more lucrative fields: the buying and selling by, the corruption of the kids from the split-level and ranch homes.

Drug abuse and addiction, robbery and assaults have come to Main Street, in our town.

There is much talk of deterrents and many arrests of drug-pushers. This should not make you comfortable or relaxed unless you are tempted not to see. The temptation is not to see how young adolescents are being encouraged and even coerced into copping out on drugs.

THE COERCION

If your child were to see clearly, he would see that the drug-pushers are tolerated and the criminals organized. Both drug-pushers and criminals, if they are big enough, are respectable.

The selling of drugs is big business—one of the biggest and most profitable. Drug companies have never hesitated to push and advertise many new and frequently inadequately tested drug products in periodicals and on TV. They also push them onto medical men.

It is sad, but sometimes physicians are pushers, and not only those who are unprincipled and crooked. Legally, too many have prescribed some of these new drugs, about which there is inadequate knowledge. Some of them have been addictive, like amphetamines and barbiturates; some of them have been harmful.

When your child goes to school he finds drug-pushing and selling within the school building and all around it on the streets. Why can't it be stopped?

When your child goes to a pizza place, a juice parlor, a dance—the joint, the pill and, the needle are there, too. Free samples are available to begin the temptation.

When you look at the courts, they are filled with small pushers; the jails, too. When you look at the legislatures, new laws are always being proposed to punish the drug-seller, and to stop the crimes in the street.

Why is drug traffic an international business? Why does the policeman who arrests the drug-user-pusher sometimes push drugs?

After you have carefully tended your children in early childhood, and worried over them as they were older, and they grew healthy enough to be 1A, why do you have to worry about their being introduced to drugs, not only in Vietnam, but everywhere the army is?

When you look at youth, yours and others, many are being quieted down. Amphetamines for behavior modification has been one of the new discipline measures in schools where there is a growing practice to ask parents to request of their physician that he provide prescriptions for drugs to quiet down the overactive, rebellious child. Was it your school where one-third of the grade-school children were receiving these stupor-producing drugs?

There is much more involved than the probability that these children will become legal addicts without their knowledge or consent. There is a move in the direction of reducing stimulation, of quieting down, of copping out on drugs, for everyone. The quiet child, the quiet youth, and the quiet man will make no trouble; each is easier to handle than the one who sees clearly what is going on and who tries to do something about it.

Turning on with drugs is turning off.

However, maybe a large addict population will just have to be endured and lived with, as automobile deaths, homicides, assaults, and alcoholism are already tolerated.

Drug proliferation, in the long run, is coercion to passivity; the passive, drugged adolescent will never be active and effective; he can never build a new world.

There is a need for young citizens to act as they have acted traditionally. There is a need for young citizens to be harbingers of change and idealism. There is a need for young citizens to be increasingly active and effective.

There is a need for young people to wish to see the world clearly and then to think clearly about it. There is a need for young people's minds to be clear and drug-free.

WHY THERAPY IS NOT ENOUGH

Therapy frequently helps young people clear up their minds. It can help relieve them of unnecessary anxieties. It can help them learn how to get along better with others. It can help them learn more about themselves. It can help them become more effective. But therapy by itself does not change the environment in which any adolescent will have to mature. Certainly, therapy can help his parents to be more effective. It can assist them in caring for him. It can help them and him in making worthwhile adjustments and even changes in his day-to-day life. All this takes place within the world, however, and if this world does not provide the opportunities and the climate that the young adolescent needs, therapy cannot help enough.

Some attention needs to be paid to the ecology of human beings, particularly the young, growing ones, because they are the resources of the world. The child's important resources are primarily in his family. When that family is troubled by unemployment, rising costs of necessities, poor housing, illness or lack of future hopes or aspirations, that child will be troubled and less effective.

The first priority must be a society that can protect its human assets by dealing with the strains inherent in today's accelerated life, by including the vital ingredients for the support of the families that raise children through meaningful work, dignified housing, and many other social and health services. Education must be related to developing individuals who walk proudly, think freely, and act wisely. There is a need for rational drug policies, for modification of laws which are excessively punitive to the individual young user and are largely unenforceable, while the biggest pushers and drug-makers go free. The laws against the individual user have to be modified and taken out of the realm of criminal activity. There is a need to police the world against the illicit drug trade and to initiate a war to end such murder, once and for all.

More has to be done, because it is no longer possible to be complacent. There is no hiding from the damage being done to the young.

There is a need for some study and planning and action and a moral commitment to clean up and clear up the social scene.

THE EPILOGUE

There are many clear-headed, clear-eyed young people. The truth is that most adolescents are not drug addicts, and there are many who are active in groups opposed to the use of drugs. These young people advocate clean living and want an opportunity to live in a clean world. Even in the slums there are those who are banding together to fight the drug-pushers. They are teaching their younger brothers and sisters that drug use is genocide. Elsewhere, young people are teaching that drug use is suicide.

Rachel Carson's *Silent Spring* has captured the interest of many young people who have addressed themselves to ecological carelessness, to the meaning of a future without the beauty and support of natural life.

There are many who are demonstrating their belief in the brotherhood of man—that no man may gorge while another starves, that discrimination is evil.

Most young people are not addicts. Many are not drug-users. All of these children, in the kinds of questions they ask, and sometimes in their discouragements, give evidence of having been brought up by good and caring parents.

These parents communicate with their young ones, listening and speaking, sharing ideals, ideas, and values. They influence and are influenced.

They help their children know who they are. They also know who they themselves are.

They are together with their children in building a better world, one that will be healthy for young and old. They want to live together in a world of hope where it will be good to have a clear mind so that all may see and enjoy what they see.

These parents and their children want a world that will be ecologically sound, peacefully safe, and humanistically oriented. They want a world that will be reassuring, a world in which it will be good to live, one in which it will be good to mature and to grow old.

Selected Bibliography

American Psychiatric Association. *Task Force Report on Encounter Groups and Psychiatry,* Washington, D.C.: American Psychiatric Association, 1970.

Blos, P. *On Adolescence: A Psychoanalytic Interpretation.* Glencoe, Ill.: The Free Press of Glencoe, 1962.

———. "The Generation Gap: Fact and Fiction." In S. Feinstein, P. Giovachini, and A. Miller, *Adolescent Psychiatry,* Vol. I. New York: Basic Books, 1971, pp. 5-13.

Blum, R. H., et al. *Horatio Alger's Children.* London: Jossey-Bass, 1972.

———. *Society and Drugs, Vol. I.* San Francisco: Jossey-Bass, 1969.

———. *Students and Drugs, Vol. II.* San Francisco: Jossey-Bass, 1969.

Bronfenbrenner, U. *Two Worlds of Childhood: United States and U.S.S.R.* New York: Russell Sage Foundation, 1970.

Brown, C. *Manchild in the Promised Land.* New York: Macmillan, 1965.

Burton, Arthur. *Encounter.* San Francisco: Jossey-Bass, 1970.

Chein, I., Gerard D. L., Lee, R. S., and Rosenfeld, E. *The Road to H.* New York: Basic Books, 1964.

Coles, R., Breener, J. H., and Meagher, D. *Drugs and Youth.* New York: Liveright, 1970.

Daedalus. "Twelve to Sixteen. Early Adolescence." *Journal of the American Academy of Arts and Sciences* 100, No. 4 (Fall, 1970).

Erikson, E. *Insight and Responsibility.* New York: W.W. Norton, 1964.

———. *Childhood and Society.* New York: W. W. Norton, 1964.

———. *Identity, Youth and Crisis.* New York: W. W. Norton, 1968.

119

Ginsbert, E. *Values and Ideals of American Youth*. New York: Columbia University Press, 1961.

Goode, E. *The Marijuana Smokers*. New York: Basic Books, 1970.

Grinspoon, L. "Marihuana," *Scientific American,* Vol. 221, No. 6 (1969). pp. 17–25.

Group for the Advancement of Psychiatry. *Normal Adolescence: its Dynamics and Impact*. New York: Scribner's, 1968.

Heyman, F. "Methadone Maintenance as Law and Order." *Society* Vol. 9, No. 8, (June, 1972). pp. 15-25.

Inhelder, B., and Piaget, J. *The Growth of Logical Thinking from Childhood to Adolescence*. New York: Basic Books, 1958.

Journal of Social Issues. "Chemical Comforts of Man: The Future." Vol. 27, No. 3 (1971).

Kaplan, J. *Marijuana: The New Prohibition*. New York: World, 1970.

Keniston, K. *The Uncommitted: Alienated Youth in American Society*. New York: Dell, 1967.

Mead, M. *Culture and Commitment: A Study of the Generation Gap*. Garden City, N.Y.: Doubleday, 1970.

Merton, R. K., and Nesbet, R. *Contemporary Social Problems*. New York: Harcourt Brace Jovanovich, 1971.

Nowles, H. H. *Drugs on the College Campus*. New York: Doubleday, 1969.

INDEX

123